PRINCETON-IN-ASIA
A Century of Service

PRINCETON-IN-ASIA
A Century of Service

REMINISCENCES AND REFLECTIONS
1898 - 1998

BY MELANIE KIRKPATRICK

PUBLISHED BY PRINCETON-IN-ASIA
CARRIE GORDON, EXECUTIVE DIRECTOR

THIS BOOK IS MADE POSSIBLE BY A GRANT FROM THE HENRY LUCE FOUNDATION

普林斯頓在亞洲

ISBN 0-9665577-1-9

Library of Congress
98-86289

Princeton-in-Asia
Princeton University
Princeton, New Jersey 08544
(609) 258-3657
pia@phoenix.princeton.edu

Designed by Rick Hibberd, New York.
Printed in Hong Kong.

論語學而篇第一

學而時習之不亦說乎

有朋自遠方來不亦樂乎

人不知而不慍不亦君子乎

THE MASTER said, 'Is it not a pleasure, having learned something, to try it out at due intervals? Is it not a joy to have friends come from afar? Is it not gentlemanly not to take offence when others fail to appreciate your abilities?'

CONFUCIUS
THE ANALECTS
Translated by D.C. Lau, 1974

FOREWORD

PRINCETON-IN-ASIA has established a long record of distinction in creating opportunities for students to live abroad and experience first hand the languages, customs and cultures of this vital region of the world. In turn, these enthusiastic young participants have given of their time and talents to help thousands of students, friends and associates in the East to gain greater insight into Western values and ideas.

Since its founding one hundred years ago, this splendid program has been an enduring force in Princeton's efforts to extend our academic mission and our commitment to human understanding far beyond campus, beyond national borders, and into the larger global community. It has survived times of war, economic turmoil and political upheaval and has flourished as an agent of peace, progress and mutual prosperity. On behalf of the entire University, I both thank and congratulate Princeton-in-Asia as it celebrates a full century "In the Nation's Service, and In the Service of All Nations."

HAROLD T. SHAPIRO

PRESIDENT

PRINCETON UNIVERSITY

*T*HE TIGERS *throughout the book are taken from Asian art, with a single exception. That is the tiger on the opposite page, which is Princetonian, sculpted in bronze. It is indigenous to the Princeton campus and can be found just outside Nassau Hall. Also found throughout the book are Chinese characters with special meaning for everyone who has participated in the Princeton-in-Asia program. The one above is the word "learn."*

INTRODUCTION

IN PUTTING TOGETHER THIS SHORT HISTORY of Princeton-in-Asia, I kept coming across a simple but profound assertion: It changed my life. This sentiment echoes across the 100 years of our history—in the archives, in interviews with former fellows, in e-mails from current interns.

Again and again throughout the past 100 years, the 1,200 young college graduates who have set out for Asia with the help of Princeton-in-Asia have been influenced by their experiences in extraordinary ways. Some ended up devoting their lives to Asia; others stayed only a year but it was often a year that turned out to be one of the most rewarding of their lives.

Some of the first Princetonians in China said it best. "The world is made smaller for one's residence in a distant place for such a period of time," wrote Samuel M. Shoemaker '16 about his two years in Peking. "One's life is never the same after such an experience." Lloyd A. Free '30 spoke of "the habit learned [in China] of getting along in a venture involving international cooperation," a habit that "has never deserted me." Franklin C. Wells, born in "Beirut, Syria" and a member of the Class of 1911, called his three years in China "the most eventful of my life."

In my own case, I wasn't an official Princeton-in-Asia fellow, but one of the informal emissaries that then-Executive Secretary Robert Atmore dispatched to Asia in the 1970s. I wanted to go to Japan, I had told him, and I eventually wanted a career in publishing or journalism. He hooked me up with Time Inc., which was looking for English teachers for a subsidiary in Tokyo. One of Mr. Atmore's innumerable contacts, it seems, was a Time executive and Princeton alumnus who was willing to consider candidates whom Mr. Atmore sent his way. My colleagues included Peter Simpson '73, Kevin Staley '75 and Nancy Broadbent '77. My students were young *sararimen* at Tokyo's major banks and trading companies. I know I learned as much about Japan Inc. from them as they learned about the English language from me. Through these young businessmen—the term Japanese businesswoman was an oxymoron back then—I also had extraordinary access to Japanese family life since many of my students invited me home to introduce me to their families. I was a young, unmarried woman thousands of miles away from home, and people were eager to make me feel welcome in their country even though they couldn't quite understand what had possessed me to go there.

These were the days when Westerners were still relative rarities in Japan, except around U.S. military bases. Even in Tokyo, people would stare and children

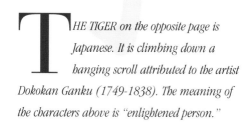

THE TIGER *on the opposite page is Japanese. It is climbing down a hanging scroll attributed to the artist Dokokan Ganku (1749-1838). The meaning of the characters above is "enlightened person."*

A Century of Service

9

would inevitably shout "This is a pen," which was, I was told, the first line in an English primer many schools used. In addition to my work at Time-Life, I moonlighted as co-host of a TV show on NHK, the national educational network, and as such gained a certain minor celebrity status among the junior-high set, who were force-fed English. When they saw me on the street, children would now shout "Hello, Melanie!" and then, "This is a pen!" I would shout back the Japanese translation: *"Kore wa baru-pen desu!"* And the children would dissolve in giggles.

Like many other P-i-A alumni, I am grateful to Princeton-in-Asia for helping to launch me on a career. In my case that is a career in journalism, at The Wall Street Journal, that has had a heavy foreign-affairs component. But most of all, I am grateful to Princeton-in-Asia for giving me the opportunity to nurture habits of mind that serve me well in every aspect of life—an openness to new ideas, an adventurous spirit, and the abiding sense that the world holds many unexplored wonders.

Many Princeton-in-Asia alumni and supporters have been generous in sharing their recollections as I collected material about our history. Some contributed essays or photos for this book and others took the time to answer my questions, in interviews, e-mails and faxes. You will come across many of their names as you read on. I thank them all.

I want especially to acknowledge Andrea Au '96, whose senior thesis on Princeton-in-Asia's early history in China was an invaluable source for Chapter One, and Wenjun Xing, whose University of Massachusetts doctoral dissertation on Sidney Gamble '12 was also a useful source on Princeton-in-Asia's formative years. Catherine Gamble Curran kindly gave permission to reprint a number of her father's extraordinary photographs of pre-war China.

Carrie Gordon, Executive Director of Princeton-in-Asia, helped me scour the archives, put me in touch with many people and passed along stories she collected. She graciously shared her knowledge of P-i-A's history and participants, which could fill a volume many times this size.

I'm also grateful for the advice of my fellow members of the Centennial Celebrations Committee—Margaret Crotty '94, Kevin Cuskley '80, Russell Da Silva '76, Karen Karp '81, Margaret Osius '77 and Anna Verdi '89. And for that of my husband, Jack David, who is a skillful editor.

As I researched the rich history of Princeton-in-Asia, I was particularly taken with the words of Donald Wallace Carruthers '15. Carruthers is typical of the young graduates who have ventured 10,000 miles away from home under the auspices of Princeton-in-Asia. Born in a little place called Beatrice, Nebraska, he went off to Peking for four years after graduation. Looking back on his experience in the late 1940s, he summed it up this way: "There is a Chinese proverb, 'I live in a small house but my windows look out upon a very large world.' My four years there had much to do with the widening of my own personal world horizons."

MELANIE M. KIRKPATRICK '73

PRINCETON-IN-ASIA (JAPAN)

Princeton Peking Gazette

12 E. 41st St.
New York

APRIL, 1927

Volume II
Number 3

SOME ASPECTS OF THE CHINESE REVOLUTION

Fourteen Points Regarding the Situation in China

A Digest of the Essential Facts, Prepared for the Gazette
by J. Stewart Burgess, '05, Professor of Sociology, Yenching University

1. The essential fact is the birth and rapid growth of a genuine national self-consciousness on the part of the Chinese people, originating with the intellectuals and spreading to all classes.

2. This new nationalism is the result primarily of Western contact and education, governmental and mission, which has brought home to the Chinese, formerly little interested in political affairs, a realization of their state of subordination.

3. The growth of this new nationalism has found intolerable the existing state of semi-independence, w...

...ts enjoyed by foreign...

for the exercise of citizenship by the people, because of the lack of economic development, and because of the millions of extremely poor and of the fact that almost 90 per cent of the entire population is illiterate, the task of nation-building is enormous.

9. Nevertheless, the thinking classes of China, who lead and dominate the masses, are a unit in the demand for an autonomous nation, and the common people rally behind these leaders.

10. It seems clear, therefore, that for the sake of the welfare of China and for the establishment of permanent friendly diplomatic relations, the eventual furtherance of foreign trade to the mutual advantage of the trading countries, and the extension of the influence of Christian enter... ...escence in the demands of the... ...the only possible wise and... ...to pursue.

Princeton Yenching Gazette

150 Fifth Avenue
New York

學 大   FEBRUARY, 1931   京 燕

Volume V
Number 1

BY WAY OF DEFINITION

WHAT? — YENCHING UNIVERSITY, at Peiping, China, now has a plant valued at $2,449,586. Its endowment and trust funds aggregate $2,211,798. Its buildings, in adapted Chinese style, have been compared favorably by a recent Princeton visitor with those of Princeton University—a compliment Yenching appreciates.

The total faculty of the University numbers well over two hundred members, and the standards of scholarship maintained by this group of teachers will compare favorably with that of our best small colleges in America. Two-thirds of the faculty are Chinese; one-third Occidentals, mostly Americans.

The enrolment has now reached 808, including 94 in postgraduate courses. These students represent the best promise of the younger generation of China.

PRINCETON-YENCHING SCHOOL OF PUBLIC AFFAIRS comprises the Departments of Politics, Economics, and Sociology in Yenching University. It has been able to gather a faculty of carefully chosen specialists in these subjects. In its courses are enrolled more than 350 of the University students. Juniors and Seniors electing these departments for their major studies num-

Mr. Chang Hung-chun, Resident Director, at his desk in our Social Experiment Center, village of Chinghe. Mr. Chang carries to this work the most thorough training obtainable in America. He is a man of tireless energy and great enthusiasm.

Political Science Club in Conference

PRINCETON-IN-ASIA is the organization's newest name and the one that has stuck the longest. The first batch of "foreign secretaries" who went "out" to Peking were collectively known as the "Princeton Work in Peking." In 1922, "Princeton in Peking" was incorporated in New York state. It briefly became "Princeton in Peiping" and then in 1930 the "Princeton-Yenching Foundation" was born, a name that lasted until 1955, when it changed to "Princeton in Asia." All these name changes have proved confusing—and even costly. Executive Director Carrie Gordon remembers talking to a Chinese-born Princeton alumnus who received a scholarship from Princeton-Yenching in the 1950s. "If I had known you were the same organization that helped me, I'd have given you more money over the years," he told her.

The logo at the top of the page says "Yenching University."

A CHRISTIAN MISSION IN CHINA
1898-1950

THE STORY OF PRINCETON-IN-ASIA begins in 1898 when Robert Reed Gailey, Graduate School Class of 1896, arrived in the northern Chinese city of Tientsin on April 26 to run the newly established YMCA. It's a measure of how important the university viewed Gailey's mission in China that it had been authorized by a resolution passed by the entire undergraduate body at a mass meeting. He was allocated $500–a considerable sum back then–raised entirely from undergraduates.

Gailey's work was sponsored by the Philadelphian Society, a popular evangelical Protestant organization on campus closely allied with the YMCA, whose first collegiate branch had been at Princeton. His mission was twofold–to spread the Christian Gospel and to help modernize China. Only two years earlier, history Professor Woodrow Wilson, speaking on the occasion of the university's 150th anniversary, had declared "Princeton in the nation's service." Now, it seemed, Princeton was determined to serve not just the nation but the world.

Gailey was a football all-American, known at Princeton as "Center-Rush Gailey" for leading the Tigers to a 25-6 victory over Yale in 1895. But he acquired a new nickname in China, where he would come to be known as "Pop" to the few dozen Princetonians who followed him there over the next four decades. He was among the wave of American Protestant missionaries who flooded China in the late 19th and early 20th Centuries as part of the Social Gospel movement. The Social Gospelers believed in both the salvation of individual Chinese souls and the salvation of Chinese society as a whole. In the case of Gailey and the dedicated young Princetonians who followed him, their effects on Chinese society, especially on education, were profound. While never losing sight of their goal of personal evangelism–or, as Gailey put it, "the moral regeneration of China's millions, one man at a time"–they also believed that it was their Christian duty to help improve social conditions in China and that their particular mission was education. They believed that the Christian message could be of practical use in solving China's enormous social problems and lifting its 400 million people out of poverty.

JESUS CHRIST AND WOODROW WILSON

"We had a Cause which gripped us," explained Richard Ritter '17, reminiscing on his years in Peking. Ritter, writing in 1973, described what motivated him and his young colleagues: "Our fundamental hope, really, was to do our little toward the birth

THE TIGER to the left is Chinese, by an unknown artist. It is taken from a leaf in a Manchu family album from the Qing Dynasty, probably the late 17th or early 18th Century. Its placement on the man's coat indicates that it is a badge, signifying a military rank. The drawing above is of Yenching University. "Virtue" is the meaning of the character.

THESE DRAWINGS (here and on the previous page) of the Princeton-Yenching School of Public Affairs originally appeared in a fund-raising booklet around 1930, hardly the most propitious year for raising money. Yet while some Princeton alumni may have been leaping out of windows on Wall Street, other alumni, faculty and students came up with enough funds to cover the new school's annual budget of $75,000.

The Princeton-Yenching School of Public Affairs was officially affiliated with Princeton University, but because Princeton's charter did not permit it to fund educational activities abroad, the task of raising and distributing money was handled by the Princeton-Yenching Foundation. The school's enrollment was 600 men and 150 women, with a faculty of American and Chinese professors teaching economics, sociology and politics. The school was one of four divisions of Yenching University, the predecessor of what is now Beijing University.

Princeton-Yenching "emphasizes a sane balance between the right valuation of the best elements in Chinese culture and the introduction of useful elements from the West," the booklet proclaims. "The earnest consideration of all Princeton men is solicited."

of a new nation. We knew that China could not go on in her old ways very much longer. We realized that she, as the largest and fundamentally one of the most civilized countries in the world, would someday be strong again; and we wanted that strength to be Christian and democratic. We believed in Jesus Christ and in Woodrow Wilson."

The 40 or so Princetonians who formed the early history of what would come to be known as Princeton-in-Asia participated in the most tumultuous period of Chinese history–from the end of the Qing Dynasty to the creation of the People's Republic. When the first Princetonian arrived in China in 1898, the Qing Dynasty was in its waning years, doomed by internal rifts and foreign pressures. Cixi, the Empress Dowager or "Iron Buddha," was the power behind the throne. A barren rock in the South China Sea known as "Fragrant Harbor" or "Hong Kong" had just been ceded to the British.

In 1900, Pop Gailey found himself dodging bullets during the anti-foreign Boxer Rebellion in Tientsin. In 1908, the year that the Princeton University Center in China was expanding its educational services in Peking, the inept Kuang-hsu emperor was dead and the disintegrating country was ruled by an infant emperor and his Manchu regents. Only four years later, in 1912, the Qing Dynasty fell, the boy emperor was forced to abdicate, and the country's future was placed in the hands of Sun Yat-sen and his fellow revolutionaries. By then, the number of Princeton volunteers in Peking was growing and a brochure of the day spoke of how Princetonians might serve the new China: "Princeton men have both a great opportunity and a well-tested medium whereby all who are interested may unite in the development and conservation of a mighty nation's greatest resource–strong young men."

The Princeton men's efforts were part of the revolutionary Christian missionary work that was transforming Chinese education with its focus on individualism, Christianity and Western ways in general. For the first 20 years, the Princeton efforts in China were through the YMCA, originally in Tientsin and then in Peking. In Tientsin, Pop Gailey ran classes for young men and established the city's first high school. In 1904, Chang Poling, a young graduate of the naval academy whom Gailey had evangelized, opened a middle school for boys that later grew into Nankai University. By a happy twist of fate, 80 years later Nankai hosted Princeton-in-Asia intern David Basson '84.

EXPANSION TO PEKING

In 1906, Gailey persuaded the Philadelphian Society to finance and staff a new branch of the Y in Peking, with Gailey and Dwight W. Edwards '04 as the "foreign secretaries." The Peking Y was officially known as the Princeton Unversity Center in Peking. Gailey and Edwards' success at running educational and recreational activities there created a demand for more help, and so in 1907 Princeton began to send more young graduates to lend a hand.

These "short-timers," as they were called, were much like the present-day Princeton-in-Asia interns. Each spent one or two years in Peking, teaching the Bible, English and history, running physical education programs, holding classes for the Marines assigned to the U.S. legation, and organizing emergency relief for natural disasters. A night school, established in 1906, offered English classes for university students and businessmen. In 1914, the Princetonians established the Peking School of

Commerce and Finance to teach English, bookkeeping, accounting and management. In 1917, Lennig Sweet '16 started an afternoon school for boy workers. Under the direction of Edwards, who stayed in China for 44 years, the Princeton University Center in Peking became a leader in famine relief work nationwide.

Princeton was by no means the only American university with a China mission; Oberlin, Wellesley, Yale and Harvard were prominent players too. In addition, then as now, the Princeton Work in Peking was not an exclusively orange-and-black operation. Volunteers from other American universities were welcome; Gailey himself had done his undergraduate work at Lafayette College. Most crucial of all, the Princetonians, a number of whom became fluent in Mandarin, relied heavily on the advice and work of their Chinese colleagues.

A notable feature of the Princetonians was their willingness, even eagerness, to exchange ideas. As early as 1906 a statement of purpose listed interaction with Chinese as one of their top goals. Cultural interchange was an essential part of all of the Princetonians' educational and community programs and the documents of the day are filled with references to "promoting Chinese leadership." The Board of Directors of the Peking Y was from the first almost entirely Chinese and Gailey made many contacts in the local business community, which he canvassed for support and money.

Back on the Princeton campus in New Jersey, the Board of Directors of the Philadelphian Society strongly believed that the "Princeton Work in Peking," the

LIFE AT PRINCETON COURT

BY RICHARD H. RITTER '17
PRINCETON-IN-ASIA (CHINA)

In 1913 the Princeton Center in Peking renovated a nearby Chinese-style mansion to accommodate the expanding Princeton staff. The house on Sui An Po Huting was divided into three sections that opened onto a courtyard. Two sections housed married staff and their families; the third served as a residence for the Princeton bachelors and was referred to as "Princeton Court."

The following is excerpted from "Memories of Princeton Court in Peking," an unpublished manuscript in Princeton-in-Asia's archives. It was written in 1973 on the occasion of Princeton-in-Asia's 75th anniversary.

Foreign visitors, on entering the court, gave little gasps of delight, congratulated us upon the beauty of our surroundings, and usually murmured something about Xanadu. We too, in our more thoughtful mode, mar-

Lunch at Princeton Court, circa 1917.

unwieldly name by which the various Princeton projects were known, would become "a rallying point for all the many religious and philanthropic enterprises already centered at Peking." The goal of the Princeton men, the Board stated, was to "advance the Kingdom of God" in every way possible. And indeed, each of the young Princetonians in Peking had his own vision of how to accomplish that goal.

Andrea Yun-Woei Au '96 calls them "Men of Faith, Men of Action" in her senior thesis on the founders of Princeton-in-Asia and stresses that the evolution of the program was "largely a function of individual initiative." She writes: "Each of these early participants subscribed to a different purpose and to a different plan of action." While they were accountable to the YMCA and to the Philadelphian Society at Princeton—and were financially supported by and to a certain extent directed by those institutions—they were largely inner-directed, initiating and carrying out projects that in their personal estimation were beneficial. The record shows that these were indeed remarkable men living in remarkable times who rose brilliantly to the opportunities set before them.

ATHLETICS IN CHINA

For Amos Hoagland '06, this mission extended to every waking hour. At work, he organized the physical education department of the new YMCA, helped set up children's playgrounds, and established China's first national athletic meets, which led to China's first participation in the Olympics. He was widely known for the personal help he provided to innumerable individuals. He paid for the education of several young Chinese men, and, as a colleague remembers, he couldn't say no to a beggar. Richard Ritter '17 wrote about his friend many years later:

"As Hoagland walked the streets of old Peking and was accosted by some filthy beggar he would say to whomever he was with at the time: 'I know that this problem is not to be solved except by social and government action, but in the meanwhile, let's stop now and do something for just this one—just this one.' And he would take 'this one' home and feed him and reclothe him...and send him out again into the streets with a smile and a 'God bless you.' "

One of Hoagland's jobs was teaching physical education at Peking Higher Normal School, where he was appalled at his students' lack of athletic ability, not surprising given that the Chinese of the day considered strenuous physical activity to be undignified. "I have never seen such lack of muscular control," Hoagland wrote of his students in his 1914 annual report. And then the ultimate insult: "They ran like young ladies in tight skirts."

Charles L. Heyniger '16 was an English instructor at Peking Higher Normal School, where he tried to encourage an interest in sports and school spirit. Soon he had his students yelling a school cheer of his own composition: "Pickety packety puck-

*FIRST "INTERN" Robert Reed "Pop" Gailey *96, posing in his YMCA uniform in a photo taken by Sidney D. Gamble '12, probably in the 1920s. Gailey is standing on the steps of the Y, whose official name was the Princeton University Center in Peking. The building was paid for by a gift from John Wanamaker, a Philadelphia department store magnate, and formally opened by Yuan Shi-kai, the day before his inauguration as President of the new Republic of China in 1912. Eighty-four years later, Yuan's great-granddaughter, Angie Yuan (Tufts '96) served as a Princeton-in-Asia intern in Shanghai.*

WHEN P-I-A'S FOUNDERS *first went to work in China, they discovered that Chinese schools had no organized athletic activities. With the arrival of Amos Hoagland '06 in 1911, all that changed. Hoagland, a football all-American, began teaching sports at the YMCA and by 1913 had established the Peking Athletic Association. "The importance of athletics can hardly be overestimated," a Princeton in Peking newsletter reported, "not only in what they may do to combat the influences of congested centers like Peking, but more far-reaching, as an aid to clear, constructive thinking which the students of today must have when in a short while they assume the leadership of a nation that is now rapidly coordinating itself into a great force." This photo shows Charles Lambert Heyniger '16 with the 1916-17 Peking Higher Normal School basketball team.*

veled at the good fortune which was ours, being supplied with quarters so refined, private, and peaceful, yet in the very heart of a great, busy city. For all of us this outward charm afforded ample reward for the inconveniences we found within.

For there were, it must be admitted, certain factors which set this Court off from the Patton, Cuyler or even Witherspoon quarters to which we had been accustomed [at Princeton]. Our floors were of stone, covered by matting. Beds were iron cots. My own was at first either the top tier or the bottom of a two-decker in which Arthur Tyler '18 and I took our turns...

Although we had never heard of ecology, this was certainly our forte, for no electricity intruded upon our simplicity, nor did motor cars, plumbing, telephones, or central heat. The oil lamps did smoke up occasionally, nor was the gaseous emission of the coal stoves desirable, but radio and television had, of course, not yet been heard of.

Don Carruthers '15 owned and played a piano and was a welcome host to any who wished to use it. I seem to remember also that he was the possessor of a phonograph, but it was seldom put into motion for records were hard to come by and rather on the scratchy side. In fact, the whole city of Peking at the time gave forth noises almost entirely human. There were no trolley cars and few automobiles. Airplanes were so scarce that we always rushed out to look if we heard one. At night the only sounds heard outside our compound were those of the watchman beating his gong every half hour or so and the melodious cries of occasional peddlers.

Our dining room, though not spacious, could comfortably accommodate 10 chairs

and their occupants, or even 12 by crowding. And it was, indeed, often crowded, for we were a gregarious lot and enjoyed our guests.

...Trolleys arrived in Peking about 1924. Well do I remember their first appearance, clanging their way amidst astonished crowds as they sped by the "Y" building on Hatamen Street...About once every five or ten minutes a car would pass us on a main thoroughfare, catapulting along in midroad at a break-neck speed of 30 miles an hour, tooting continuously as it went. Pedestrians as well as rickshaws, wheelbarrows, bicycles, palanquins, donkeys, camels, two-wheeled carts, even wedding and funeral processions, would flee to the safety of the side paths as the cars raced by. Rickshaws were abundant, comfortable and cheap.

...Most of us at Princeton Court taught, some of us full time, in Walter's [Walter Young, Graduate School Class of 1917] Commercial School, and also in the English Night School. In one of my evening classes I had what must have been the last boy in Peking to wear a queue. At least he was the last in the "Y" school and this school tended to be more conservative than government schools. Although he was terribly embarrassed by it and tucked it as inconspicuously as possible inside of his gown, papa had said he must wear it, and that was that! The other students seemed to be sympathetic with him, and I also sensed that they were also somewhat respectful of the father's solid conservatism. I never noticed that Yang was "kidded" about it. In those days, respect for parents, teachers, and indeed all elders, was deep. When we teachers entered our classrooms, all the students rose, bowed deferentially and waited to be seated until we had gestured our permission.

...It will have dawned by now, I think, upon any readers who may have perused this paper to this length that Princeton Court enjoyed a dozen facets to its life style. We possessed, perhaps, some of the aspects of a monastery, for we were a group of men living together if not under rules at least under the custom of obedience, chastity, and poverty. No one of us even so much as thought of breaking through the conventions of our Princeton Center morality. No one was seriously tempted toward "high living," or sexual experimentation. Marriage was something for the future. As for poverty—though certainly not poor by Chinese standards—we lived at a pretty bare minimum and we all had an equal salary. We could receive medical care from mission doctors free (though I do not remember any of us as ever having been seriously ill). We paid no rent, and our traveling expenses to and from our American homes were defrayed; and then we had the consciousness that if anything serious happened to us, our families would be behind us. Otherwise we lived the life of the money-free and accepted it without demur.

...Happy we are that Princeton's work still continues after these more than 75 years of service! Our present-day young graduates are scattered among many universities in the Far East; Princeton Court is gone; the "Y" is a communist organization; and Yenching has become the central unit in the largest government university in the country. In other forms and in some cases under other ideologies we still believe, however, that our work is continuing. All of us must have the faith to trust that Princeton's services and ideals have not been for naught. 🐎

ety pool/Peking Higher Normal School!" The archives offer no indication as to whether this poetic encouragement led the athletes on to victory.

John Stewart Burgess '05 took the Princeton Work in yet another important direction, social work, with the establishment of the Peking Social Service Club in 1912. This was the first of many such clubs he organized and later nurtured into a larger program of community service. Under Burgess's leadership, the Princeton Work expanded to include numerous social services–opening playgrounds, editing neighborhood newspapers, finding jobs for ex-prisoners, conducting public hygiene campaigns.

Burgess was also the inspiration for the Princeton Work's most enduring project–a monumental sociological study of every class of Peking resident, from rickshaw men to members of the literati, conducted by Sidney D. Gamble '12 and a team of Chinese researchers, whom he and Burgess trained. "Peking: A Social Survey" was published in 1921 to wide acclaim in the U.S, where no less an authority than the philosopher and educator John Dewey called it "indispensable to further studies of China." Burgess became the first Princetonian to teach at Peking (Union) University, the predecessor of Yenching University, setting up a sociology department there in 1919.

Gamble, who also taught at Yenching, went back and forth between the U.S. and China through the early '30s. Not only was he an effective go-between for the Princetonians in Peking and Princeton University, he also was the chief fund-raiser in the U.S., a task that grew harder as the Depression set in. From 1929 until his death in 1968, Gamble was president of Princeton-in-Asia and all its predecessors. It's fair to say that without his energy and dedication, Princeton-in-Asia would have died out long ago.

P RINCETONIANS in Peking, 1932. From left to right: Richard H. Ritter '17, Lawrence M. Mead '11, Robert Duncan '25, Dwight W. Edwards '04, Lennig Sweet '16, Randolph Sailer '19, Harry Price.

YENCHING UNIVERSITY

By the late teens and early '20s the Princeton Work in Peking was shifting to higher education, thanks in large part to Burgess's growing ties to Peking (Union) University. An explicit goal of the Princeton Center in Peking had always been to train Chinese men and women to take over the American missionaries' work. By the early 1920s the Princeton men at the Y had done such a good job that Burgess and others recommended that Princeton turn the YMCA over to local management and focus its efforts on Peking (Union) University. In 1926 the university changed its name to Yenching, after an ancient literary name for Peking. It was the predecessor of what is now one of China's most prestigious institutions of higher education, Beijing University.

Befitting its new focus, the Princeton Work in Peking also got a new name. "Princeton-in-Peking" was founded in the U.S in 1922, taking over supervision and financing of the Princeton projects in Peking from the Philadelphian Society, whose support on campus was diminishing along with the general decline of religious fervor. The separation from the Philadelphian Society also reflected a shift in the underlying aim of the Princeton Work in Peking from evangelization to education.

The Board of Trustees of the newly incorporated Princeton-in-Peking voted in 1922 to concentrate its resources on Yenching, a decision that was endorsed by the Princeton University Board of Trustees in the following year. In 1928, Princeton-in-Peking briefly became Princeton-in-Peiping, when the capital moved to Nanjing and "Peking," the "northern capital," saw its name changed to "Peiping," or "northern peace."

By 1930, the transfer of resources and personnel to Yenching was complete, and Princeton-in-Peiping got a name that would stick for the next 25 years–the Princeton-Yenching Foundation. This organizaton, headed by Sidney Gamble, was set up with the express purpose of funding the Princeton Yenching School of Public Affairs. Its trustees were then, as now, mostly alumni of the program and professors at Princeton, with the President of Princeton serving in an honorary role. By now, Princetonians had been teaching at Yenching for more than a decade, focusing on political science, sociology, social work and economics. In 1928, Edward Corwin, a noted political science and international law professor at Princeton, did a stint at Yenching as a visiting lecturer. He was just one of a number of prominent Princeton faculty members who taught at Yenching in the '20s and '30s, just as Yenching professors taught at Princeton and other U.S universities.

The new school had considerable support back at Princeton University, which

THE GAMBLE LEGACY

By Catherine Gamble Curran
Princeton-in-Asia Lifetime Trustee

My father always said he was "bitten by the China bug" in 1908, when his parents took him to China for the first time. That visit, to Shanghai and Hangzhou by way of Honolulu, Japan and Korea, left him with a lifelong love of Asia. Just to show you how utterly different siblings can turn out to be, as a result of the very same trip that enthralled my father, his older brother vowed never again to leave the United States—and he never did.

My father, however, made three more lengthy visits to China—1917-19, 1924-27 and 1931-32. It was on the first of these that, at

*S*IDNEY D. GAMBLE '12 *and his Smith Corona, 1917. When Gamble and two friends traveled up the Yangtze River into Sichuan Province, 15 men carried them and their 17 pieces of luggage in sedan chairs, a common mode of travel in those days.*

Sidney D. Gamble '12 and Walter S. Young '16, probably in the late 1910s.

the request of John Stewart Burgess '05, he researched his monumental study of the lives of ordinary residents of Peking. His book, "Peking: A Social Survey," was published in 1921. On his subsequent visits he continued his social research, enlisting the aid of a team of Chinese researchers, whom he trained, and publishing extensively on urban and village life in China. "How Chinese Families Live in Peiping" was published in 1933. By then he had become president of the Princeton-Yenching Foundation, the precursor of Princeton-in-Asia, a position he held until shortly before his death in 1968.

Throughout his sojourns in China, my father traveled widely, always taking his camera with him to record the lives he witnessed around him. He took thousands of photographs—and stored them away in the attic of our house in Riverdale, New York, where they rested comfortably until the early 1980s, their historical and artistic value unsuspected by anyone in our family.

The recovery of his photographic archive came about quite by accident. Of course, as we were growing up, my two sisters, my brother and I were well aware of our father's interest in photography. Family expeditions would see him draped about with cameras and light meters, and one or the other of us was often delegated, not without protest, to help carry some of the equipment. And of course I had leafed through his books and glanced at the photographic illustrations, but I hadn't the experience or the knowledge to realize what a priceless legacy they represent.

So it came as a complete surprise, sometime in the early '80s when I was attending a meeting in Princeton, to see projected on a

wall some beautiful, strangely colored transparencies of Chinese scenes identified as "Sidney Gamble's Magic Lantern Show." It seemed that the recently appointed executive director of Princeton-in-Asia, Jason Eyster '74, had been looking into its history and had repeatedly come across my father's name. He made an appointment to talk to my mother and, during the interview, was directed by her to a closet on the third floor of the house where he found rosewood boxes containing several hundred hand-colored glass slides and shoe boxes stuffed with what turned out to be nearly 6,000 black and white negatives.

With the help of foundations, friends and colleagues, I spent the next several years having the collection catalogued and many of the people and places identified, including those in the Gamble photos included in this chapter. The result was an exhibition that traveled under the auspices of the Smithsonian Institution Traveling Exhibition Service to 19 cities in the U.S. and Canada. Yale historian Jonathan Spence has called the Gamble photographs "vigorous, unsentimental, and starkly, yet never cruelly, illustrative of the deep and real suffering that lay at the heart of China's long revolution."

There is an old saying: "It is a wise child that knows its own father." I think and hope that I am wiser now than I was. I have looked at China through my father's eyes and through the eyes of his camera. I have shared his youthful enthusiasm and his joys of discovery, appreciated his quiet humor, admired his persistence and determination and been moved by his idealism and humanity. ➤

had recently opened its own School of Public and International Affairs (later the Woodrow Wilson School) and which considered the Princeton-Yenching School its "Far Eastern laboratory." A brochure of the day explained the university's interest in its Chinese outpost: "The same spirit which has determined the historical development of Princeton has brought about this extension of its influence in public affairs beyond the border of America." The ties between the two schools were extremely close, and over the next seven years, the university sent numerous students and professors to Yenching. The Princeton-Yenching Foundation raised money for Yenching's beautiful new campus, a grouping of Chinese-style buildings and gardens near the old Summer Palace in the western hills of Peking.

A booklet published by the foundation stated the school's goals: "Yenching emphasizes a sane balance between the right valuation of the best elements in Chinese culture and the introduction of useful elements from the West. It emphasizes equally cooperation between the Chinese and American faculties. It seeks to constitute an international society in miniature."

Despite the increasing political turmoil, the Princeton Yenching College of Public Affairs grew rapidly in quality and stature. Graduates became prominent in government, education and vital public relief programs such as rural reconstruction. Yenching University survived the Japanese occupation in 1937, only to be closed down when the U.S. and Japan went to war in December 1941. In 1942, the university was re-established in the city of Chengdu in far western Sichuan Province, the students and faculty having walked the 2,000 miles from Peking. Among the faculty were the indefa-

SIDNEY D. GAMBLE '12 awakes at Princeton Court. In an essay on Gamble's work, historian Jonathan Spence writes of Gamble's three perspectives on China: "first, his deep conviction of the relevance of Christian teaching to China's plight; second, his training in social sciences and economics, which enabled him to accumulate data that would engender creative changes; and third, his love of photography, which would add the camera's eye to his own effort to focus on the crisis of his time."

tiguable Dwight Edwards, now approaching his 40th year in China, and Professor Wu Chi-yu, a Princeton Ph.D., who headed the social science work of Yenching-in-Exile.

At the end of the war, Yenching was the first university to be re-established in north China and classes were resumed in 1945 at the badly battered campus in Peking. "Then the Communists rolled in," Sidney Gamble relates in a later account. The Christian university continued to operate under Communist rule and "we were criticized for supporting work in a communist controlled area, but we felt we should not desert our fellow workers who were carrying on the same educational program that they had earlier." Yenching was "liberated" in December 1948 and as late as October 1949 the Princeton-Yenching News reported that "officials in Peiping have made it clear that Westerners are welcome to stay and carry on their activities."

Not long after those reassuring words, Sino-U.S. relations worsened and the Communists expelled the Americans working at Yenching. Yet, ever hopeful that the Communists would allow the university to operate freely, Princeton-Yenching continued to send money, assuring its supporters that "no PYF funds go to support courses in communism."

The Princeton-Yenching News of November 1950 carried an article by a down-hearted Randolph T. Sailer '19. Professor Sailer had taught psychology at Yenching for 30 years under the auspices of the Presbyterian church, survived the war in a Japanese detention camp, and, like so many of the Princetonians who had lived in China, held great affection for the country. He was ardently looking forward to the day when he could return. There is "complete religious freedom on campus," he assured his readers. And, "I know personally many intelligent, earnest, fair-minded men and women in Communist China," he wrote. "Now we are separated from them not only physically but by walls of propaganda."

By Christmas the U.S. and China were at war in Korea. There would not be another Princeton-in-Asia representative in mainland China until 1980.

A NEW BEGINNING
1950-1970

The Princeton-Yenching Foundation now faced a crisis, possibly an insurmountable one. Communist China was closed to the world and the Christian Yenching University was in the process of being transformed into the state-run Beijing University, under a government that was officially atheistic. After more than 50 years of supporting education in China, the organization could no longer fulfill its mission.

Or it had to redefine it.

The first obstacle to that goal was the organization's own Board of Trustees, which was deeply divided over what to do next. As unlikely as it might sound at the end of the 20th century, in the early 1950s it was by no means clear that the Communists were there to stay–or if they were, that they would long remain at odds with the U.S. Hope remained that the Princetonians could soon return to their work at Yenching, the country they loved, and the friends and colleagues they cherished. Toward that end, the Board sought vainly to stand apart from the politics of the day. As late as February 1950, the minutes of a Board meeting refer obliquely to "this very trying time" and show that the Board voted to dip into its reserves to provide extra financial support for Yenching, which was still trying to get back on its feet "after the war." Princeton University formally severed its relationship with Yenching in February 1951.

THE TIGER *on the opposite page is Korean, carved into the roof structure of a rural temple. "Practice" is the meaning of the character.*

SCHOLARSHIPS AND PROPAGANDA

By June of that year the Princeton-in-Asia Board, under the continued leadership of Sidney Gamble, decided to inaugurate a scholarship program for Chinese students at Princeton and elsewhere. In doing so, the Board was very much aware that the Princeton-Yenching Foundation's cross-cultural goals worked in two directions; its aim was both to educate young Chinese leaders and to educate young Americans about China. By sponsoring Chinese students at Princeton and elsewhere, it hoped that the American students would benefit as well. Among the recipients of the scholarships were Robert Wei '53, Eugene Wong '55 and Paul Woo '56.

In 1952, worried about the spread of Communism into other parts of Asia, Princeton-Yenching threw its support behind a propaganda program aimed at promoting democratic and Christian values among Chinese in Southeast Asia by placing articles in local newspapers, magazines and other media. The "Literature Project," as it was known, was established under the auspices of the United Board for Christian Colleges in China and was headed by former Yenching Professor T.J. Ku.

AN FUTURE SENATOR'S INTRODUCTION TO CHINA

BY BILL BRADLEY '65
PRINCETON-IN-ASIA (TAIWAN–HONG KONG) FROM "TIME PRESENT, TIME PAST" (KNOPF, 1996)

After the [1964 Tokyo] Olympics, I toured Asia under the sponsorship of a program called Princeton in Asia, which sent recent Princeton graduates to teach in a few non-Mainland Chinese colleges. I was a gold medalist and a forthright Christian, and people apparently wanted to hear about both experiences. I went to Taiwan, where I spoke at Tunghai College and heard whispered comments from students about governmental efforts to inhibit open debate. At the U.S. embassy in Taipei, I cast my first ballot for president, voting for Lyndon B. Johnson. In Hong Kong, I spoke at Chung Chi College, walked the narrow alleys of Kowloon City, bought a tailor-made sports jacket, and ate my first Peking duck at the favorite restaurant of Chung Chi's President Andrew T. Roy. Dr. Roy, whose parents had been missionaries in China and whose son would later become U.S. ambassador to China, told me that few in Washington understood either the dangers or the opportunities that China represented for the United States, and that no one fully appreciated China's potential economic dynamism. When he spoke of his early years in China—about the people he knew and the communist terror that followed—tears welled up in his eyes. Later I would read about Mao's genocide immediately after assuming power, and about the excesses of the Cultural Revolution, and I would remember Dr. Roy's face in that Hong Kong restaurant in 1964.

Above: Bill Bradley '65.

I N 1981, Charlie Stevens '63 and Owen Nee '65 (in the plaid pants) tracked down the old Princeton Court in Beijing and discovered that it had been turned into a Communist kindergarten. The building is believed subsequently to have been torn down; at least no recent P-i-A-er has been able to locate it in the sea of glass-and-steel structures that now occupy the area.

A front-page essay in the Princeton-Yenching News of November 1953 assesses the Literature Project's first year in what it called "the struggle for the minds and hearts of Chinese in Southeast Asia" and reports that the project's anti-communist articles had been published in "Formosa, Malaya, Singapore, Hong Kong, Burma, North Borneo, the Philippines, Indonesia, Thailand, Sarawak, Cambodia and Vietnam." It concludes: "In this strategic part of the world, a basic conflict between two faiths is taking place, the outcome of which will be of importance not only to Asia but to the peace of the world." The history of Southeast Asia over the next two decades would prove this to have been a prescient comment.

Both the scholarship program and the Literature Project were viewed as temporary measures—worthy uses for the foundation's money and resources until the future course could be determined. As the months passed the prospect of returning to China became more and more remote and the future of Princeton-Yenching became no clearer.

In particular, the Board was deeply divided on the question of "Formosa" or Taiwan, where the Nationalist government had fled in the wake of the Communist takeover of the mainland. The subject of establishing a program in Taiwan was formally raised for the first time at the June 1952 Board meeting when one of the younger members, William Fenn *48, proposed that the foundation support a new college that was being established in Taiwan. According to the minutes of that meeting, Mr. Fenn believed Tunghai University in Taiwan could be a "logical substitute" for Yenching.

A heated discussion ensued. The venerable Dwight Edwards '04, one of the founders of Princeton's program in China, was opposed, fearing that an association with an institution in Taiwan might have "unpleasant effects" on Princeton's Chinese friends still on the mainland and that it might prevent the resumption of the founda-

tion's work there. Another senior member, Timothy Pfeiffer '08, expressed his vigorous opposition to any investment in Formosa "for political reasons" and "because of the insecurity of the island." The motion was defeated.

*J*OHN HALEY '64, teaching freshman English at International Christian University in Tokyo. ICU, like many Japanese universities in the 1960s, was at times closed down by disruptive student demonstrations. Here students barricade ICU's main building in January 1966.

With Taiwan too hot to handle, the Board turned its attention to other Asian countries. In 1953 it approved grants for colleges in South Korea and Hong Kong, both of which, like Tunghai, were supported by the United Board for Christian Higher Education in Asia. In Seoul, Chosun Christian University (now Yonsei University) received money for scholarships and books, and in Hong Kong, Chung Chi College (now the Chinese University of Hong Kong) received funds for its library. In both cases, the grants marked the beginning of fruitful relationships that would last for many years. Also in 1953, Princeton-Yenching subsidized the salary of a Yenching professor, Y.P. Mei, who spent a year at Princeton's philosophy department. Dr. Mei had been acting president of Yenching when it was in exile in Chengdu.

TUNGHAI UNIVERSITY

Nevertheless, in June 1953, a year after the tumultuous Board meeting of 1952, the Board approved a tentative first step toward Taiwan. It allocated $5,000 for the purchase of books in the field of public affairs at Tunghai University. But it wasn't until 1955 that the Board threw its whole-hearted support behind the new university. At the same time, Princeton-Yenching took a step that paved the way both for its support of Tunghai and for its future development: It changed its name.

On September 9, 1955, the Princeton-Yenching Foundation officially became Princeton in Asia, when the New York Department of State, from which the organization had received its original charter in 1922, gave its approval. In explaining the

R ICK JOHNSTON '64, in a series of photos from Tunghai University in Taiwan in the mid-'60s. They illustrate the life of a typical intern then and now: teaching, performing community service, and playing sports. While Rick's main job was to teach English at Tunghai, he also volunteered to teach at a local middle school for girls and participated in student work camps, where Tunghai students and teachers dug ditches, painted walls, and cleaned sewage canals in nearby villages. And he was occasionally roped into a student-teacher athletic event such as the tug-of-war pictured here; that's Roger Mills '65 tugging behind Rick.

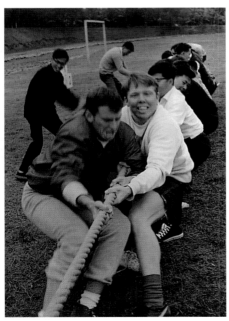

trustees' decision, the organization's newsletter reported with characteristic understatement that "PYF had been out of contact with Yenching since December 1951 and saw little prospect of an early renewal of the relationship that had such a long and honorable history."

The article concluded: "In changing its name, Princeton in Asia is not breaking away entirely from its past. It is assuming a title which more accurately describes the new era in which it proposes to continue its efforts to train democratic leadership in Asia." The hyphens in the new name, by the way, didn't emerge until the '60s.

Tunghai, located in central Taiwan near the city of Taichung, opened in the fall of 1955 on a new campus designed by I.M. Pei. A cable announcing the fact reads: "BY GRACE OF GOD A CHRISTIAN UNIVERSITY IS BORN IN FREE CHINA." Just as three decades earlier Princeton-in-Peking had funded the new Yenching College of Public Affairs, the newly named Princeton-in-Asia voted $7,500 to support a public affairs college at Tunghai. The money was directed to be used for books, scholarships, faculty salaries, a "Princeton Room" for seminars, and a Princeton-in-Asia chair for a leading professor in the social sciences. The first holder of the chair was Wu Teh-Yao, a mainlander who was an expert in international relations and a former member of the Republic of China's delegation to the United Nations. Professor Wu went on to become president of Tunghai. To understand how far $7,500 could go in Taiwan in the mid-1950s, consider that $2,000 paid for Professor Wu's salary and $500 covered the tuition of five students.

THE FIRST 'FELLOWS'

Tunghai holds a special place in the history of Princeton-in-Asia, for it was here that the current internship system took hold. In 1959, the university became host to the first official postwar teaching fellow or, as we call them today, intern. And so, a decade after the last Princetonian was forced out of China, William Volckhausen '59, renewed the tradition of young Princetonians setting off to work, teach and, above all, learn in Asia.

Gary Martin '60 joined Bill Volckhausen the following year, and by 1961 the two-year fellowship at Tunghai was so popular at Princeton that there were 10 applicants for the job. Over the next 30 years, Princeton-in-Asia would send 47 fellows to work and study at Tunghai, helping to build it into one of Taiwan's most respected universities. Writing in 1998, Olivia Chang, a lecturer at Tunghai, remembers fondly "those outstanding young men and women" who "came into Taiwan like a breeze of fresh air. Their dedication and performance was impressive. The influence of their interaction with the students and the people in Taiwan, as I see it now, was positive and enormous. Their friendships with the local people and among themselves were lasting. It is safe to say that they taught us as much as they learned from us."

Bill Volckhausen may have been Princeton-in-Asia's first "official" postwar fellow, but the title of "first fellow" rightly belongs to two enterprising students who made their way to Japan in the summer of 1958. Jackson Huddleston '60 and Hamilton Meserve '59 set off for Tokyo with the encouragement of a Princeton professor and the promise of help from Yoshio Osawa '25 and his son Zenro Osawa '57. This was the beginning of the Osawa-Princeton Club of Japan summer fellowship, which continues today. More than 70 Princeton students have been introduced to Japan through this program and it remains one of Princeton-in-Asia's most sought-after assignments.

At Princeton in the early 1920s, Yoshio Osawa was nicknamed "Seaweed" Osawa, after the crates of seaweed that his mother would ship him from Japan. Russell Da Silva '76, who was an Osawa fellow in the summer of 1975, remembers Zenro telling him about his father's affection for Princeton; the elder Osawa was proud that he had contributed to the university's annual giving fund every year since graduation–even during World War II when such remittances were seemingly impossible. After the war, he was dedicated to improving U.S.-Japan relations. He invited the entire Class of 1925 to Japan in the 1950s for a reunion, and then, in 1958, started the summer program that became the Osawa-Princeton Club of Japan internship.

The fellowship programs expanded quickly in the 1960s–to Hong Kong, Japan, South Korea, Singapore and (briefly) Indonesia. In 1963, John McCobb Jr. '61 was the first teaching fellow at Chung Chi College in Hong Kong's New Territories. John Haley '64 went to Tokyo in 1964 to teach at International Christian University. Paul Minault '68 taught at the University of Indonesia and in 1969, Christopher Binns '69 was dispatched to Korea University in Seoul. The following year Bruce Stone '70 went to teach at Nanyang University (now the National University of Singapore) in Singapore. The fellows mostly taught English but also economics, literature, political science and American studies.

At the time that these young graduates were working and studying in Asia, the Asian Economic Miracle was only a gleam in entrepreneurs' eyes. In the 1960s, the tiger economies were all still undeveloped and the Princeton-in-Asia fellows lived under much the same conditions that their colleagues did–which is to say, very modestly. A hamburger, if one even existed in the towns where the fellows lived, was an unaffordable luxury–the stuff of daydreams or, if a guy got lucky, a treat from a resident Princeton alumnus at the local Hilton.

Owen Nee '65 was a fellow at Chung Chi from 1965-67. "There were no phone calls home," he remembers. Worse, there was no indoor plumbing during the year he lived with his Chinese teacher in a little house in Hong Kong's New Territories. (It may have been worth it; Owen's Chinese is fluent.) Writing for the Daily Princetonian in 1963, Peter Pugh '60 reports that his salary as a Tunghai fellow was $1,500 a year plus a $2,000 travel allowance and a summer of Chinese language study. No one ever accused the Princeton-in-Asia fellows of being in it for the money.

POLITICAL TURMOIL

These were the Vietnam War years, and many contemporaries of the young Princeton-in-Asia men were seeing Asia from behind the barrel of a gun. While the rest of Asia was at peace, the political turmoil spread throughout the region and the fellows weren't isolated from it. In Taiwan, fellows noted the curbs on free speech when the subject of mainland China was raised. In Hong Kong, the fellows at Chung Chi could go to the top of a nearby hill and look out at inaccessible Guangdong Province. In Japan, the late '60s were a time of violent student demonstrations, often

TENNIS WITH THE CROWN PRINCE

BY JACK HUDDLESTON '60
PRINCETON-IN-ASIA (JAPAN)

On a cold February night in 1957, Ham Meserve '59 and I were discussing Professor Robert Butow's history course on Japan and China. We had gone to high school together and also been exchange students to England. Americans could not travel to China, but why not go to Japan for the summer? Thus began the post-war Princeton-in-Asia. For 16 frustrating months, we tried with Professor Butow's help to get to Japan, involving along the way Professor William Lockwood and Dean Ernest Gordon of the Chapel. At one point, Professor Lockwood commented, "It's a shame that this campus isn't vacated more often for such worthwhile projects." Finally, on July 5, 1958, we boarded a Pan Am Clipper in Los Angeles and headed for Tokyo.

Yoshio Osawa '25, president of the Princeton Club of Japan, had assured Professor Butow that if we could get to Japan, the club would arrange a six-week stay in Tokyo—with English teaching to cover our expenses, two weeks of travel throughout Japan, as well as weekend trips. The problem was that a round-trip plane ticket from L.A. to Tokyo cost $850 in 1958—the equivalent of more than $5,000 today.

We both worked over the summer of 1957 to cover the cost but still fell short. Endless letters to presidents of U.S. airlines, the secretary of the Navy for military transportation, and shipping lines finally resulted in a job on an Italian tanker going to Indonesia via Nagasaki. My mother did not like that one bit. Unfortunately, the tanker was rerouted and we were again without transportation. We decided finally to buy plane tickets from the West Coast and

Zenro Osawa '57.

arranged through AAA to drive two rather unpleasant ladies across the country from my home in West Virginia. Together, Ham and I were off to a world that would play a major part in our subsequent lives.

Upon arriving in Tokyo at 7 a.m. on July 7, we were met by Mr. Osawa's son Zenro Osawa '57, served a second breakfast, briefed over lunch by members of the club, and treated to cocktails with a very colorful alumnus. All within six hours of arrival. No thought of jetlag. After that we never had a spare moment. We stayed in the help's quarters of the International House of Japan the entire summer for $1.53 a day, including breakfast, and received $3 for transportation, lunch and dinner—plenty in those days if you like curry rice and beer, as I do. That summer there was a drought and, being without air-conditioning, we often concluded the evening sitting on the roof of I-House drinking beer and watching the all-night construction of Tokyo Tower. Any winnings at pachinko were pooled for cigarettes for me and candy bars for Ham.

Our students were various: a nine-year-old girl, an elderly medical scholar, the two sons and half-brother of the then-Foreign Minister, and the Censorship Bureau—where

Ham saw the films before they were censored. The following year the lucky interns taught geisha!

Ham is a superb tennis player and I get by, so we played a lot of tennis, including the Karuizawa tournament where we were photographed being watched by the Crown Prince. My roommates were impressed when they went to the movies in Princeton in November, when the prince's forthcoming marriage was announced, and saw us on the newsreel. We were staying in Karuizawa with a friend who didn't have hot water, so after our matches we ambled over to the Osawas' new resort home and asked if we could take a shower. Mrs. Osawa graciously invited us in; we showered and became the first dinner guests in their lovely new home. We hadn't realized that dropping in unexpectedly simply wasn't done in Japan, but without Mr. and Mrs. Osawa, there would not have been a summer program then nor for the next 40 years.

A two-week trip at the end of the summer took us to Kyoto, where we enjoyed a tea ceremony performed on a miniature boat by Grandmother Nomura, the wife of the founder of the Nomura Group; to Hiroshima, a city of construction dust where people stared at us, often tittering in embarrassment; and finally to Beppu—100-degree heat and a Tom Collins without ice, accompanied by a fish head. No thanks!

Forty years later, two Princetonians still go to Japan for the summer on a Osawa Princeton Club of Japan grant. Ham stayed on and worked for a year for the Japan Times and subsequently in Tokyo, Taipei, Seoul and India for Citibank; he was also president of Princeton-in-Asia. I made a living working mostly in Japan and the rest of Asia, became Bob Butow's colleague at the University of Washington teaching on Japan-related topics, and incidentally married a Japanese lady. Ham's son Chris and my daughter Saya, like the children of Bill Volckhausen '59 (the first intern in Taiwan), have been on Princeton-in-Asia. I hope at least one of my three grandchildren will also—perhaps in Mongolia. 🐎

What's That Carp Doing in My Bathtub?

By William A. Volckhausen '59
Princeton-in-Asia (Taiwan)

My lifelong association with Taiwan began with a room full of empty chairs. In the fall of 1958 I had been named director of the Princeton Summer Camp in Blairstown, N.J. for the summer of 1959. My main job during the winter was the identification and hiring of the camp's staff. On a cold night in mid-November, I was scheduled for dinner with Chapel Dean Ernest Gordon and a group of students who had expressed interest in the camp. Unfortunately, someone had forgotten to send out the invitations and the dean and I dined alone. During the conversation I mentioned my interest in teaching outside the U.S. after the summer camp was over.

A week later as I nursed a cold in my dorm room, I received a visit from the dean and Richard N. Pierson, both of the Princeton-in-Asia board. During the course of the visit I was offered the job of teaching English language and literature for two years at Tunghai University in Taichung, Taiwan, Republic of China. Since Taiwan seemed to have the requisite distance from home and lack of familiarity, I was persuaded quickly that I should accept. The only problem: the Communist shelling of the offshore islands of Quemoy and Matsu had convinced my parents that going to Taiwan would be to place myself in harm's way. Much discussion followed–leading to a compromise: My parents would bless my acceptance of the P-i-A position and I would approve my father's purchase of a $2,000 life insurance policy on my life to be used to pay to ship my body home in case I didn't make it. I am pleased to report that the insurance policy has never been used for its original purpose.

After studying Mandarin Chinese with Professor Fritz Mote during the spring and summer of 1959 and reviewing Chinese-character cards on the 3 a.m. drives back to the Princeton Summer Camp from New York City Shakespeare Festival performances, I arrived in September in Taiwan able to carry on a reasonable conversation in Mandarin. What I was not at all prepared for was that on my arrival in class all of my students rose and bowed as one as I reached the platform in the front of the room. I was completely stunned and asked the students not to do that again. You must remember that some of the students were older than I was.

The school at which I taught, Tunghai University, was opened in 1955 in Taichung, Taiwan, home of the U.S. Army Chinese Language School. Tunghai had been placed at this spot in the center of the island of Taiwan to represent the effort to foster peaceful relations between the Chinese from the mainland and the Chinese who had lived on Taiwan for 300 years (the Taiwanese).

A P-i-A family: Bill Volckhausen '59 (Taiwan), Sharon '91 (Korea), Grace, and Alex '93 (Singapore).

The university had been created out of a sweet potato field on the hills overlooking the city of Taichung and looking further east to the high mountains running down the center of the island. From my point of view, this location was good because it provided easy access to the network of roads that connected the farm villages covering most of the land between the university and the Strait of Taiwan about 20 miles to the west–and, of course, the People's Republic was still further west over the horizon.

Quite often on a weekend afternoon, a small group of students would gather on the campus and then spend the rest of the day tramping out and back to one of the not too distant villages. A cold or wet weather alternative to hiking was the old-fashioned dumpling party, when students would gather in my living room with all the fixings and in two to three hours would turn out several hundred delicious dumplings that would sustain life for a considerable period.

For a group of about 10 of us, these weekend hikes culminated in a three-day hike from the ridge atop the mountains of central Taiwan down the Toroku Gorge to the East Coast. The walk was memorable because of the wild, undeveloped beauty of the steep, sharp mountains as well as the road itself, much of which had been blasted out of the sheer granite face that rose almost straight up from the sides of the river. We spent the third day exploring the quiet East Coast town of Ilan.

Turning to indoor life, I am happy to report that teaching at Tunghai afforded much opportunity to develop close personal relationships with faculty and students. I shared a small house with another American bachelor. Our house was blessed by the presence of Mrs. Chen from Beijing who was a wonderful cook and who spoke near-perfect Mandarin. To display Mrs. Chen's skills we would frequently entertain at dinner parties. Early in my tenure we scheduled one such party for a Saturday night. Imagine my surprise when at 4 p.m. I walked into the bathroom to take a shower only to discover a large carp swimming happily in my half-full bathtub. "That is tonight's dinner," explained Mrs. Chen. "We Chinese like our fish really fresh." The moral of the story: Shower in the morning of your dinner party.

During these dinner parties, I also learned the special rules governing the playing of mahjong in Taiwan. Since the government had declared mahjong illegal on the island because it encourages gambling, we had to prepare for our games by closing all the windows (in a tropical country!), pulling down the blinds and putting a heavy blanket on the game table to absorb the sound of the clattering tiles. (We didn't gamble and just had a lot of fun.)

My Princeton-in-Asia experience had a strong influence on many of my most important life decisions. Most important was my marriage to Grace Lyu, a Korean-American. It also led to a master's degree in modern Chinese history, several years of legal practice with MFY Legal Services in Chinatown in New York City, and long-term service on the boards of directors of the Asian American Legal Defense Fund and the Asian American Federation. The next generation of Volckhausens has received the P-i-A genes, with our daughter, Sharon '91, interning in South Korea (1991-92) and our son, Alex '93, in Singapore (1993-94). As for joining Jack Huddleston's grandchildren in P-i-A (see Jack's nearby article)...we'll see.

in protest of the large American military presence there.

James Aliferis '69 arrived in Tokyo after a summer of intensive language study to the news that International Christian University wouldn't open that September due to a student strike. He never was exactly sure what specifically the students were striking about, even though they managed to close the university for a couple of months. Jim remembers the protracted negotiations between the ICU administration and the protesters, who had barricaded themselves in a dormitory. When the talks foundered, ICU next cut off water and electricity to the dorm. Finally, Jim remembers, the university "announced a date certain in November when school would open, erected a 12-foot high solid steel fence around the central buildings on ICU's bucolic campus, and posted large notices that anyone not attending classes or using force to stop those who did so would be at risk of immediate arrest and expulsion." Students returned peacefully to class and Jim had to work overtime so that the seniors could graduate in April as scheduled.

While Princeton-in-Asia's focus was firmly on the new fellowships, it also pursued several other cross-cultural projects in the 1960s. In the autumn of 1964, it sponsored the Asia tour of the Class of 1965's most famous member–basketball star Bill Bradley. Princeton-in-Asia sent him to Taiwan and Hong Kong after he had won an Olympic Gold Medal at the Tokyo Olympics. The future Senator spoke at Tunghai and Chung Chi and also taught basketball clinics. According to a newsletter of the day, he told students that "Communism is out of date and too small for today's world." Andrew Roy, president of Chung Chi, took the trouble to write the young Olympian's mother in Crystal City, Missouri, after his visit. He included just the sort of news a mother could be expected to want to hear: "I met him at the airfield," he said. "He needed sleep, but was in excellent physical condition."

On campus, Princeton-in-Asia participated in several exchange programs. In 1969, with funding from the Japan Society, it sponsored the visit of two editors from the University of Tokyo Press for six months of training at Princeton University Press. And it arranged for two civil servants from Singapore, then a very new country, to study public policy at the Woodrow Wilson School. In addition, it expanded its role in putting Princeton professors and students in touch with their counterparts in Asia and vice versa.

As the 1960s ended, Princeton-in-Asia's transformation into the organization that it is today was well under way. In 1968 Executive Secretary David Harrop '55 made a lengthy trip to Asia (cost: $2,794.13) to seek new opportunities for young graduates. Mr. Gamble, who had been president of the organization since 1929, passed away in 1968. The Board of Trustees declared that Mr. Gamble's "able guidance, his enthusiasm, his generosity, his pleasant personality and his persistence

K IT BINNS '69, with the Korean family with whom he lived in Seoul while at Korea University. This photo of the Kim family was taken on the occasion of Tae-hyon's graduation from 8th grade in 1971.

Princeton in Asia News
Succeeding Princeton-Yenching News

VOLUME XXIII MAY 1956 NUMBER 2

Wu Teh-yao Occupies PIA Chair at T...
Six Stud...

PRINCETON IN ASIA NEWS

PAIK, CCU PRESIDENT, STUDIED AT PRINCETON

(Two years ago and again this year, Princeton in Asia has sent $2500 to Chosun Christian University, Seoul, Korea, for scholarship aid and books. CCU, Korea's oldest university, is 41 years old.)

L. George Paik, President of Chosun Christian University in Seoul, Korea, secured a Th.B. degree from Princeton Theological Seminary in 1925 and an M.A. from Princeton in the same year.

Dr. Paik has been president of CCU for the past ten years. He joined the institution in 1927 as an assistant professor. Following Pearl Harbor, the Japanese took over Chosun Christian College and "dismissed" faculty and staff.

After the liberation of Korea in August 1945, a group of former staff members, including Dr. Paik, formed a committee to recover the property and reorganize the faculty. Dr. Paik was named president in January 1946. Shortly thereafter, the college was granted university status.

The ten years of Dr. Paik's presidency of CCU have been turbulent ones for Korea. On many occasions he has been called upon to serve his government in Korea and abroad. For one period of nearly three years he was on leave from the university to act as Minister of Education. He has also been a leader in a ...

Stories of PIA Scholars at CCU Illustrate Tragedy and Fortitude of Korea of Today

Four students at Chosun Christian University in Seoul, Korea, are receiving scholarship help from a gift of $1000 made to the University by Princeton in Asia, Inc. President L. George Paik of the University outlines the personal stories of these students, which illustrate vividly the upheaval and tragedy of life in Korea during the past fifteen years, and Korean determination to carry on as possible.

San Mo Chung is the son of In Po Chung, one of the finest Chinese scholars in Korea, who was one of the original members of the faculty of Chosun Christian University. He became a captive of the Communists in the summer of 1950, and we have heard nothing of him since. The second boy, San Mo, has tried to support the family of seven; they have no house to live in and no source of income. San Mo, who had only one more semester to complete his course, felt he had to drop out in order to support the family. One Princeton scholarship will go to this boy and enable him to finish his course.

Chosun Christian University has, despite wars and occupations, grown to an enrolment of 2300 and now comprises seven colleges and the graduate school. A year ago first steps were taken toward merging CCU and Severance Union Medical College...

P-1-A KOREA SCHOLARS

FROM "PRINCETON IN ASIA NEWS"
MAY 1956

Four students at Chosun Christian University in Seoul, Korea, are receiving scholarship help from a gift to the University made by Princeton in Asia, Inc. President L. George Paik *25 of the University outlines the personal stories of these students, which illustrate vividly the upheaval and tragedy of life in Korea during the past fifteen years, and the Korean determination to carry on as possible:

San Mo Chung is the son of In Po Chung, one of the finest Chinese scholars in Korea, who was one of the original members of the faculty of Chosun Christian University. He became a captive of the Communists in the summer of 1950, and we have heard nothing of him since. The second boy, San Mo, has tried to support the family of seven. The family is abjectly poor; they have no house to live in and no source of income. San Mo, who had only one more semester to complete his course, felt he had to drop out in order to support the family. One Princeton scholarship will go to this boy and enable him to finish his course.

Miss Heiran Lee is a senior majoring in English language and literature. She is the second daughter of Soon Taik Lee, who was a director of the Commercial department of this college for many years, and one of the leaders in the field of economics and commerce in Korea when our Government was organized in 1948. When the Communist invasion took place he was captured and we have heard nothing about him. He left behind a family of six children, wife and mother-in-law. The oldest girl gave up her studies and is employed; Heiran also has tried to earn as much as she can. As a student, she maintains good records; as a campus leader she has served as President of the Women's Student Association. She went to the country last summer leading the evangelistic team of women students for work among rural women.

Seung Moo Lee is a senior student in chemistry. He is the son of an alumnus who died some years ago. The widow had to raise three children, of whom Seung Moo is the eldest. Mrs. Lee, a college graduate herself, has a little fruit stand in a shack on the Severance compound. During the war Seung Moo joined the army, but returned to finish college. He stands at the top of his class.

Miss Oak Sook Choo is the daughter of a former navy chaplain of Korea who has been jobless for some while. She was one of the brightest girls in her high school, and came to us last spring, without taking entrance examinations because of her outstanding record. But her parents could not pay her registration fee. At the end of the semester she stood second in her class. She is majoring in philosophy, but has many-sided interests. One of the Princeton scholarships will go to her.

have been major factors in [Princeton-in-Asia's] creation and development and the increase of its program."

A SECULAR ORGANIZATION

That same year Princeton-in-Asia published a booklet outlining its programs and announcing plans to expand its fellowships and summer work programs. The new president, Alfred Howell '34, wrote: "In this report you will read of new countries and their universities where we wish to send young Princeton men to teach and live with their Asian counterparts." His report made no mention of a Christian mission. While some of the universities with which Princeton-in-Asia had connections were founded by Christians (as, of course, had been Princeton), the stated goal of the organization was no longer to spread the Gospel. It was "to promote interchange of people and ideas" and to contribute to Asian education.

By the time the '60s ended, Princeton-in-Asia had a part-time, paid Executive Secretary; growing support among Princetonians in Asia (both Asians and the few Americans who were working there); an office on campus; and exploding interest among the undergraduate body.

In short, Princeton-in-Asia was poised to take off.

J ACK LANGLOIS '64 (left) and Rick
Johnson '64 make their debuts on Taiwan
television during the 1972 New Year
Festival. They are dressed up as traditional
Chinese comics – wearing long robes or changpo
and carrying fans – and are performing a
cross-talk routine called xiang-sheng. Jack and
Rick, P-i-A fellows in Taiwan in the 1960s, were
back in Taiwan doing Ph.D. research.

THE ATMORE MAGIC
1970-1982

HERE'S HOW Robert C. Atmore described Princeton-in-Asia's assets in 1970, the year he became the organization's first full-time Executive Secretary: "I looked at the foundation's resources," he told the Princeton Alumni Weekly in 1981, "which were a $300,000 endowment, a room, heat, a typewriter, a respectable history, and Princeton. The trustees and I figured we should be able to send a lot more people to Asia."

They were right. By the time Mr. Atmore retired in 1983 the program had expanded to about a dozen countries and roughly 40 participants, broadly the same shape it currently takes, which is to say, big enough to make an impact but small enough not to lose its personality.

How did it happen? The short answer is two words: Bob Atmore, whose energy and enthusiasm built Princeton-in-Asia into the program it is today.

Princeton-in-Asia was a second career for Mr. Atmore, who had spent 35 years at the Choate School in Connecticut as a librarian, teacher and housemaster. Physically, he was a man much like Pop Gailey, the first Princeton-in-Asia fellow, who was so tall he had to have an oversized rickshaw custom-built for him in Peking. But while Gailey looked smart in his military-style YMCA uniform, Mr. Atmore favored the rumpled, academic look for his tall, slightly stooped figure. He had an occasional stutter that was severe enough to make those who knew he had once taught public speaking wonder at the personal determination and strength of character he must have possessed to master it as well as he had.

THE TIGER to the left is Japanese, of the Muromachi Period. It sits at the side of one of the 16 disciples of Buddha. "Joy" is the meaning of the character.

MORE CONVERTS THAN BELIEVERS

Writing at the time of Mr. Atmore's death in 1995 at the age of 82, Marius Jansen '44, Japanese history professor emeritus at Princeton, spoke of his remarkable rapport with students and how he encouraged them to risk an encounter with Asia. "He was more interested in converts than believers," Professor Jansen writes. "My colleagues and I were sometimes disappointed that he seemed to give preference in assignments to students without experience and language study, instead of seeking out our majors. But Bob reasoned that the majors were sure to go, whether he sent them or not; it was more important to get new people involved. Those with some language and background he encouraged to go on their own, by whatever means available; once there, he assured them, they would find their slot. And he was usually right."

In keeping with his aim of casting as wide a net as possible, Mr. Atmore managed to get a number of unlikely candidates interested in Asia, particularly Japan, through jobs he set up there with Japanese companies. One example is Richard Obermann '71, of the Engineering School, who spent a summer as an apprentice at Yasakawa Electric Co. in Kyushu and wrote about his experience for the Winter 1972 Princeton Engineer magazine: "It's becoming clear that the reemergence of China and the growing economic and technological strength of Japan will make them increasingly important contributors to future political and technical developments." Bear in mind that this line was written in 1972, the year Nixon went to China, before Hondas and Toyotas had taken over American highways and before the invention of the Walkman. A summer in Asia had clearly taught Dick Obermann a useful thing or two.

THE 1970s saw the start of a number of business internships at Japanese companies, including two popular summer ones: Matsushita in Osaka and Nikko Securities in Tokyo. Craig Forman '82 is the fifth hard hat from the left.

JOBS IN JAPAN

Mr. Atmore also found opportunities for students to study Japanese management up close, most notably at Matsushita Electric Co., where, in 1972, he set up a summer program. The popular Matsushita internship, the annual selection for which became hotly contested on campus every spring, lasted until 1992 and dispatched 40 interns to Osaka.

It wasn't always easy for the young Americans to understand Japanese customs, but there's no question that they learned. Eve Lesser '77 told the Daily Princetonian in 1976 about her summer working for Matsushita: "One of the hardest things we found to adjust to was that the society was oriented to the group, not the individual. If we finished a task early (3:30 in the afternoon), we couldn't leave until 5:15. You can't leave when other members of the group are still working–it's not fair to them."

Japan was by far the most popular destination for Princeton-in-Asia interns in the 1970s and, thanks in part to the efforts of the growing Princeton community there, many opportunities opened up. The teaching job at International Christian University (ICU) kept going, as did the Osawa-Princeton Club of Japan summer fellowship. In addition to these positions, Mr. Atmore put interns in jobs in Kyoto, Toyama, Hiroshima, Kumamoto, Kanazawa, Shizuoka, Odawara and elsewhere outside the Tokyo metropolis. Most of these positions weren't "official" P-i-A fellowships but rather the serendipitous matching of willing students and needy institutions by Mr. Atmore.

The experience of Ruth Stevens, Kirkland College '72, shows how the Atmore magic worked. Mr. Atmore helped Ruth track down a job in Kanazawa, an ancient city on the west coast of Japan, where she taught English at the local technical high school. As was typical, Mr. Atmore kept in touch, and when Ruth decided to spend the summer studying Japanese at a language school in Tokyo, she offered her "life"– apartment, friends, private teaching jobs, Japanese art classes–to a Princeton-in-Asia intern of Mr. Atmore's choosing. "Three Princeton women took over my Kanazawa life while I was in Tokyo for successive summers," Ruth remembers. And so another internship was born.

There are dozens of Princeton-in-Asia alums from the Atmore era with similar tales to tell. Thanks to Mr. Atmore, David Edwards '75 ended up in one of the world's most desolate places, Kabul, Afghanistan. From 1975-77 he taught at the American Center there, courtesy of a connection Mr. Atmore had made with a senior official in the U.S. Embassy who had attended Princeton.

Mr. Atmore was also a prolific correspondent. He tracked down Princetonians in Asia or with Asian connections and cajoled them into helping the young people he was dispatching overseas. And once a young man or young woman reached Asia, he or she would be sure to hear from Mr. Atmore. He pecked out letters on a rickety old typewriter in Palmer Hall or just scrawled a note and stuck it in an envelope. These were the days before photocopiers, and he would use a dittograph machine to run off copies of his reports and newsletters–which he mailed to a widening circle of supporters and funders. To save money on postage, he'd send a packet of letters to Jackson Huddleston '60 in Tokyo and ask him to forward them to addresses in Asia.

CLEARING HOUSE ON ASIA

Along the way, Princeton-in-Asia became a kind of campus clearing house on Asia. Tristan Beplat, an active trustee and banker with extensive contacts in Asian financial circles (among other jobs, he had been on the U.S. team that had set Japan's postwar exchange rate at 360 yen to the dollar), organized career panels for students to explore job opportunities in Asia. Tris also enthusiastially helped a number of Princeton students find banking jobs with Asian connections.

Students with an interest in going to Asia would make a point of stopping by 224 Palmer Hall for advice, whether or not they wanted to apply for an internship. S. Gail Buyske *79 remembers consulting Mr. Atmore before leaving for a job in Hong Kong with Chase Manhattan Bank; she got back a long, handwritten letter and a list of phone numbers.

During this period, the formal internships at Tunghai, Chung Chi and Nanyang also continued, and other informal positions started up in Taiwan, Hong Kong and Singapore, often with the help of a local alumnus and/or the local Princeton Club. Mr. Atmore was nothing if not persistent; in the parlance of the '90s he'd be known as a

Bob and Edith Atmore in the early 1950s.

ROBERT C. ATMORE

BY SCOTT D. SELIGMAN '73
PRINCETON-IN-ASIA (TAIWAN)

I met Bob Atmore in 1973, in the final months of my senior year. Like many other seniors, I had waited until just about the bitter end to decide what my future ought to be. I recall fondly my first interaction with Bob: I asked him if he was Mr. Atmore and he told me to go away and come back the next day. Which I did.

I realized only several years later that injecting obstacles in people's paths was part of Bob's strategy for sifting out the seniors who were truly serious about going to Asia from those who were merely casting about for something to do after graduation. I apparently passed the test because Princeton-in-Asia, largely on his say-so, selected me for a fellowship at Tunghai University in Taiwan. My parents were dead set against it, but Bob had a chat with them because he knew instinctively that the experience would do me good. What neither of us had any way of knowing at the time was how profoundly that decision would change my life. And how much richer it would be as a result.

Throughout my time in Taiwan, and for many years afterward, Bob was someone to whom I turned for career counseling and good, old-fashioned advice. He was always willing to listen and could always draw on his wealth of experience and come up with something both smart and helpful to say. I doubt he ever had any training as a guidance counselor, but that's probably what made him so good at it. He was a natural.

One of the things I liked the most about him was his joie de vivre. He just seemed to enjoy people, and enjoy himself, so much. He was a man who counted his blessings and who brought out the very best in others. ✦

WE HAD EVERYTHING TO LEARN

By Dori Jones Yang '76
PRINCETON-IN-ASIA (SINGAPORE)

When my brother graduated from college in 1966, his biggest concern was to avoid going to Southeast Asia. So he was pretty amazed, in 1976, when I headed straight for that part of the globe, two weeks after graduation from Princeton. So were the others in my family, not known for venturing far from our roots in northeastern Ohio. Nobody expected the youngest daughter of the Jones family to fly off to Singapore. Maybe that's why I did it.

The three of us who went to Singapore in 1976 were typical of the graduates Princeton-in-Asia targeted: None of us knew much about Asia, so we had everything to learn. Tom Pyle '76 was well-known at Princeton as the head of student government, and Bruce Von Cannon '76 was a widely admired tennis ace. I had spent most of my waking hours at The Daily Princetonian. But despite Princeton's excellent East Asian Studies program, we had all majored in something else—in my case, European history. I had taken only one Asia-related course-- "Asian Politics," focusing on one country per week for a semester. Before I left, someone taught me to say *"Ni hao ma?"* but those were the only words I knew in Chinese.

In Singapore, I was met at the airport by Mary Tay, a gentle, wise teacher of English at Nanyang University, where I was to spend two years. She became my neighbor and trained me in the ways of teaching English as a second language. Our students had graduated from Chinese-language schools, and most felt insecure about their English. I was only a few years older than the girls and the same age as most of the boys.

An odd confluence of Great Power Politics met in our Chinese classroom. Our teachers were all Mandarin-speaking Chinese. About one-third of the class was American, one-third Japanese, and one-third Russian. The Soviet Union, in those years, couldn't train its China scholars in either China or Taiwan so the only choice left was Singapore. Every Friday the Russian students went off to their embassy for vodka and propaganda. They also were apparently assigned to get to know us Americans through soccer games and occasional parties. Among the American students, always, was a guy from the "State Department," who took a special interest in getting to know the Russians.

DORI JONES YANG '76 on R&R from Singapore in Malacca, Malaysia, in 1977. Like most P-i-A interns, Dori took the opportunity of living abroad to visit as much of Asia as possible. An unofficial requirement of a internship is to offer sleeping space on the floor to interns visiting from other countries.

Four hours a day, five days a week, in the classroom for two years...that, I realized, is the best way to learn a language as difficult as Chinese. Still, after two years of intensive study I visited Taiwan and was hard-pressed to say such simple things as "I want to pay for my room now." It took two more years of language study in graduate school and another of evening classes in New York before I was comfortably fluent.

The highlight of my Princeton-in-Asia experience, though, was not in the classroom but on the road. With a salary of only $200 a month, I barely scraped by. But fortunately, my housing and Chinese classes were free, and Princeton-in-Asia provided not only airfare but an additional stipend of $500 for travel. That was enough to underwrite two years of excursions, with a backpack and "Southeast Asia on a Shoestring" guide, to Java, Bali, Sumatra, Malaysia, Brunei, Sarawak, Philippines, Thailand, Burma, Hong Kong, Japan, Korea and Taiwan, as well as a going-home trek through Nepal, India, Pakistan, Afghanistan, and Iran. (Yes, I hit Afghanistan six months before the Soviet invasion and Iran six months before the Shah fell. My dad was clenching his teeth the whole time.)

From the insides of jeepneys, pedicabs, and tuk-tuks, I could see enough of Asia to know I wanted to learn more. So I spent the next two years getting a master's degree in international relations at Johns Hopkins. As luck would have it, Deng Xiaoping visited Washington D.C. during those years and China opened up to American journalists. Foreign editors were looking for journalists who could speak Chinese and understood Asia; I nabbed a job at Business Week. After 18 months of training in New York, my editors there gave me the biggest break of my life: a plum assignment as the Hong Kong bureau chief, when I was 28 years old, covering China, Taiwan, Hong Kong, and all of Southeast Asia. I went for a three-year assignment and stayed for eight years, watching China open in ever more fascinating ways.

My P-i-A experience changed my life—and Tom Pyle and Bruce Von Cannon can no doubt say the same. My husband, Paul Yang, was born in China and raised in Taiwan; we were married in Hong Kong and held our wedding reception in Macau. Tom Pyle, too, married an Asian, Molly, from Singapore, and worked as a banker many years in Korea and Hong Kong. Bruce married a Chinese woman from Taiwan, San-San, and has lived and worked in Taiwan and Singapore.

If the goal of P-i-A is to improve Americans' understanding of Asia, it sure worked for this Ohioan. My daughter, Emily, can say her earliest immigrant ancestors came to America in 1640 and her latest, her Chinese grandma, arrived in 1991. Today in Seattle, she lives, every day, with the flavors of a continent that for me, back in college, seemed only an exotic dream. 🏃

champion networker. The jobs in Taiwan were often sought by East Asian Studies majors who wanted to perfect their Mandarin in the expectation that mainland China would soon open up to Americans.

Alexander Kelso '71 was the only Princeton-in-Asia fellow to teach at Catholic High School in Singapore, where he went in 1972. He taught English to 9th- and 10th-graders, including the son of then-Prime Minister Lee Kuan Yew. Lex remembers being criticized for his "unconventional" teaching methods, which encouraged the kids to speak and ask questions, something in the style of Princeton's famed preceptorials. The criticism ended when his students came in first in the national English exams. "It's weird but it works," his colleagues concluded. Phillip Witte '79 taught English literature at Srinakharinwirot University in Bangkok, where he remembers taxi drivers driving barefoot and his apartment having running water only five hours a day.

Mr. Atmore forged a number of long-lasting internships at Gadjah Mada University in Yogyakarta, Indonesia; the Korea Development Institute in Seoul; National University in Singapore; and Srinakharinwirot University in Bangkok. He started Princeton-in-Asia's on-again, off-again placements in India (obtaining visas has been a particularly vexing problem there) and its program in Macau at the University of East Asia (now the University of Macau).

The Atmore years also saw the expansion of the program into the Middle East and, for some now obscure reason, Greece, where the program sent 10 interns between 1974 and 1989. Mr. Atmore's geographical definition of Asia was elastic, to say the least, and under his direction, the program grew to include internships in Eqypt, Iran, Afghanistan, Kuwait, Jordan, Lebanon, Turkey and Yemen.

A number of these programs were short-lived; Terry Wrong '80, for example, saw his internship in Beirut cut short in 1981 when a mortar took off the roof of his school. But others, most notably in Egypt, lasted for many years. Fifteen interns taught there between 1978 and 1990, when the trustees halted the internship due to the Gulf War. Most of the Egypt internships were at the American University of Cairo, working in various administrative offices.

Princeton-in-Asia fellows have often found themselves in the middle of history as it was being made. So it was for Frank Packard '81, who arrived in Cairo in September 1981, three weeks before the assassination of President Anwar Sadat. His apartment wasn't far from Sadat's residence and troops, expecting trouble, massed beneath his balcony. Presidents Nixon, Ford and Carter attended the state funeral that followed, a sign of American respect that, Frank remembers, "brought immense joy to every Egyptian I met in the days that followed. Truly, Americans appeared to be unable to do wrong. Subsequent to the assassination, surprise military roadblocks were common, but the sight of an American passport opened all doors and cleared up any concerns."

Virginia Vogt '77 was one of only two interns to go to Yemen with Princeton-in-Asia. It was a classic Atmore story. She wandered into 224 Palmer Hall with the notion of going to Japan and, *voila!*, left planning to go to Yemen. It seems Mr. Atmore had an old friend who was the deputy chief of the U.S. mission there; he arranged a job for her at World Airways and a home with a Yemeni family in Sana, the capital.

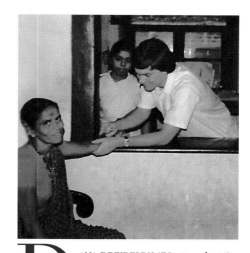

D ANA DREIBELBIS '78 at work at St. Luke's Hospital in Vengurla, India, in the summer of 1976. Vengurla is the hometown of former Princeton President Robert Goheen '40, then-U.S. Ambassador to India. St. Luke's had been founded by President Goheen's father in the early 1900s. On July 4, 1976, when Americans were celebrating the nation's bicentennial, Dana was in Vengurla, plowing a rice paddy with a water buffalo.

From left (standing), Dirk Peterson '79, Ken Egusa *83, Craig Forman '82, and Charlie Diao '79 with Matsushita colleague Hiroshi Kosaka in Osaka.

ON BECOMING FLUENT IN SMILING

BY CRAIG FORMAN '82
PRINCETON-IN-ASIA (JAPAN)

Students who enter the Princeton-in-Asia office on the first floor of Palmer Hall often wind up halfway around the world. As an intern at the Matsushita Electric Industrial Corporation outside of Osaka, Japan, I was in a program designed to teach college students about Japanese business philosophy and to point out differences between Japanese and Western business practices. For eight weeks we participated in seminars on Japanese management policy, discussing a range of issues from superior-subordinate relations to the division system of corporate organization. We talked about corporate labor unions, the consensus method of decision-making, and the lifetime employment system. We toured company plants and worked on the production line at the Matsushita Dry Battery Company. In short, we were introduced to the life of the Japanese worker.

The six of us—one German, one Canadian, two electrical engineers from Holland, Ken Egusa *80, and I—spent a 40-hour work week at the Matsushita Overseas Training Center, asking and answering questions and occasionally writing reports about what we saw. On weekends we traveled to Kyoto or central Osaka to visit museums and shrines, shop at department stores, and frequent the ever-present beer garden. Everywhere we went the sheer numbers of people were striking.

Even so, I found I stood out in a crowd. All the young kids would stare at me because I was a *gaijin*, a foreigner, but I learned to be flattered by their good-natured curiosity and became fluent in smiling. Though I spoke little Japanese, the communications gap was gradually bridged.

Once the Kyoto train station manager tried to explain to me how to return to the dormitory where Matsushita housed its interns. I knew that the trip required a change of trains, but my smile told the manager that I had absolutely no idea what he was telling me to do. Taking me by the arm, he led me through the station to the proper train and gave the engineer a sharp order. As we pulled out, he waved and said, "Bye, bye." At my connection, the engineer brought the train to a stop, led me to the appropriate platform, and put me on the second train. Then he spoke to the engineer and waved as it pulled out. At my final destination I got off the train amidst the nods and smiles of my fellow passengers, who had become aware of my plight, and headed back toward the engineer to thank him. But as I walked along the platform, the train began to pull out and the engineer smiled, waved and said, "Bye, bye."

I learned something about Japan, I guess: certainly enough to know I could never make an accurate generalization about the people or their customs. I learned to overcome my desire to know at all times what we were doing next, and my hesitancy to be led around to yet another sight whose significance remained unexplained, or at least uncomprehended. I discovered that sharing experiences with friends was satisfying enough. And I found that it is not hard to live in other societies and cultures whose ideas, customs, and language are different from your own. All you need is a comfortable pair of shoes, a change of clothes, an open mind, and a smile. 🐎

Reprinted from Princeton Alumni Weekly, January 12, 1981

Ginna remembers a situation she faced that you can be sure Pop Gailey never encountered:

"The bright dresses worn at the parties were in sharp contrast to the outfit women were expected to wear in the street: the *sharshiff*, a black covering originally imposed on Yemenis by conquering Turks. To the great dismay of my [Yemeni] family, I once tried the garment out. Even the mother, who was an extremely traditional woman, told me it was 'evil.' The *sharshiff* is designed to cover every part of your body. First, you put on a long black skirt which sweeps the ground; then you wrap a long black elastic cloth around your head, neck and lower face which is followed by a shawl which covers your head, upper body and arms, falling down below the waistline; finally you attach the double-layered veil which covers the remainder of your face and head. I don't know how Yemeni women managed walking in the *sharshiff*, because I couldn't see a thing through the double thickness of the cloth. To keep from falling, I had to walk along with my head tilted in such a way that the veil fell forward, exposing the patch of ground directly at my feet."

BACK TO MAINLAND CHINA

It was during the Atmore years that the first Princetonians took up the mantle of Pop Gailey and returned to mainland China as teachers, both through formal Princeton-in-Asia internships and through personal arrangments, often with the encouragement of Princeton-in-Asia and the East Asian Studies Department.

One of them was Madelyn Ross '79. In what may be the only recorded example of a poor judgment call by Mr.

Atmore, Madelyn recalls that he originally discouraged her from trying to work in China–though she is quick to note that he stayed in touch once she got there thanks to the help of Professor J.T.C. Liu, a Princeton-in-Asia trustee. She arrived at Fudan University in Shanghai in August 1979 and spent the year teaching and studying. Madelyn remembers hooking up with Lorraine Spiess '78, who was teaching in Beijing; running into Scott Seligman '73 at the Friendship Store in Beijing; and attending a Christmas party for Princetonians given by J. Stapleton Roy '56, who was working at the newly established U.S. Embassy. (He later became ambassador to China, Singapore and Indonesia.)

By a fluke, the first official Princeton-in-Asia fellow in China was not from Princeton but Harvard. Princeton-in-Asia President Charles Stevens '63 paid a visit to Beijing Normal University in the spring of 1980 with the purpose of lining up a job for a Chinese-speaking fellow or fellows there. Back at Princeton, graduation day came and went with nothing decided. Finally, in June, Charlie reached an agreement with BNU. By then, no Princeton students were available and so Mr. Atmore contacted Harvard, which introduced him to Steve Persky, who had just graduated. Steve and Mr. Atmore met for drinks at the Algonquin Hotel in New York and six weeks later he was on a plane for Beijing.

To say that the first China fellowship was disorganized would be an understatement. Mr. Atmore gave Steve an address, a phone number and the name of a contact person but stressed that he had no idea what conditions would be like. No one met Steve at the airport and since it was the weekend no one at university even answered the phone. A man he had met on the plane took pity on him and put him up at his hotel overnight. On Monday, he wandered over to BNU.

In his letter to BNU sealing the deal, Charlie Stevens had noted that BNU would provide housing for the fellow in "regular" dormitories. "We do not wish for any Princeton-in-Asia fellow to be isolated from Chinese students or society," he wrote. (Foreign teachers previously had lived off-campus at the Friendship Hotel.) And, indeed, living conditions were basic, Steve remembers, with hot showers available only three times a week and meals taken in an open-air student cafeteria, which meant no one lingered over dinner in January. There were no phones in the dorms. The second Princeton-in-Asia intern at BNU, Elizabeth Frank '81, tells of having to use the local mail to set up weekend dinners with friends who lived just across town. This was remiscent of the days of Pop Gailey at Princeton Court–only he had servants to deliver his communications.

As Steve Persky's selection indicates, Princeton-in-Asia had by now opened up to non-Princetonians. This was another Atmore innovation and appears to have started in

O*ff-off-Broadway at Tunghai University, Scott Seligman '73 directs his students in "Fiddler on the Roof." A few years later Susan Danoff '75 produces "The Crucible."*

ROBBIE BROWNE '71, Jonathan Hines '74 and Pat Patterson '74 grace the photo at the top of the page. It's from a custom-made postcard they sent Bob Atmore in the fall of 1974. The three have set aside their workaday business suits for yukata, or cotton kimono, which they wore to a Halloween party near Mount Fuji, seen in the background. Robbie, Jonathan and Pat were teachers at the Institute for International Studies and Training, where they taught culture as well as language, including such vital social skills as how to mix drinks and give toasts in English.

Two other teachers in Japan — Melanie Kirkpatrick '73 (center left) and colleague, and Alyssa Short Poincenot '79 (below) — learn to wear kimono, tie obi and necessarily walk in very short steps. Alyssa is wearing traditional wedding attire, including a wig, in a picture that made its way into a Kumamoto newspaper.

1972, when Mr. Atmore founded the Asian-American Intercollegiate Placement Service, a coalition of colleges that agreed to cooperate in sending students and recent graduates abroad. This organization, which receives only glancing mention in the archives, seems to have fizzled out by the end of the decade, but Princeton-in-Asia continued it in spirit, welcoming applicants from other universities, as it does today.

LOW COSTS, HIGH RETURNS

Despite its rapid growth, Princeton-in-Asia continued to operate on a shoestring budget. The university graciously supplied office space in Palmer Hall. The endowment, which had been built through Sidney Gamble's generosity and hard work, provided a modest income. Under Mr. Atmore's fund-raising efforts, the base of supporters began to grow, relying heavily, as before, on alumni and faculty, but now also on the growing number of Princetonians in Asia, both Asian graduates of Princeton and American alumni who were living there. An Advisory Council was established in the early '70s, composed mostly of Princetonians in Asia.

A promotional brochure breaks down the costs for 1974: $13,800 for seven teaching fellows (at Tunghai, Nanyang, Chung Chi, and ICU) and to help defray the expenses of four Asian scholars at Princeton; plus $16,500 for office expenses, postage and Mr. Atmore's salary, all of which contributed to sending an additional 49 young Americans to Asia. With the exception of the designated interns at Tunghai, Nanyang, Chung Chi and ICU, some of whom received a travel stipend, students usually had to come up with their own air fares. The institutions they worked for provided a small stipend and, in most cases, a place to live.

Speaking to the Princeton Alumni Weekly in 1981, Charlie Stevens described the life of a typical intern: "P-i-A people don't live as expatriates in golden ghettoes; they live as ordinary people would. They have been doing that for more than 80 years, and though their reasons for doing so have changed, the results have essentially remained the same—forging a bond with another culture that transcends time and distance."

By 1983, the year Mr. Atmore retired, Princeton-in-Asia looked much as it does today, only far less structured. That informality worked well in the '70s and into the '80s, thanks in large part to the strength of Mr. Atmore's personality. It was also due to the fact that the East Asian economies were taking off and there were plenty of opportunities for adventurous young Americans who wanted to teach English and were willing to live on the local economy.

But Asia was changing and Princeton-in-Asia had to change with it.

princeton
ALUMNI WEEKLY
JANUARY 12, 1981

Princeton-in-Asia Since 1898

Princeton-in-Asia has been a favorite topic of the Princeton Alumni Weekly over the years. Professor John M. Warbeke '03 wrote an article about Yenching University titled "On a Pagoda-Studded Campus" for the February 26, 1932 PAW. He wrote: "I wish I had a million dollars to help foster the work that is here literally saving the world. Let no Princetonian forget that the alma mater is still a strategic power here in China."

INTO THE FUTURE
1983–PRESENT

"**W**E WERE RATHER MORE INFORMAL IN THOSE DAYS," recalls Marius Jansen '44, professor emeritus of Japanese history and a Princeton-in-Asia trustee, speaking of the '70s and '80s. The Atmore model held steady through most of the 1980s, under the leadership of Executive Directors Jason Eyster '74 (1983-1985) and Barney Williamson '43 (1985-89).

With an annual budget of roughly $50,000, by the late 1980s Princeton-in-Asia was sending as many as 100 students and young graduates abroad. The actual costs of the individual positions continued to be borne three ways, as they are today: by Princeton-in-Asia, which matched up students and institutions; by the fellow, who usually paid his or her travel costs; and by the host institution, which typically provided housing, language classes and a small salary. (For a few fellows at schools that couldn't afford the necessary stipend, Princeton-in-Asia would supplement their pay.) The $50,000 in expenditures was raised from the interest on the $500,000 endowment and annual fund-raising.

There were, however, significant differences from the Atmore years. First, several of the Asian universities with which Princeton-in-Asia had longstanding fellowships outgrew the program; they either had competent local staff available or now required teachers with advanced degrees. But there were plenty of new openings to take the place of the ones that ended, and the late '80s was a period of growth, most notably in South Korea and Thailand. In Korea, positions were established at the Korea Herald and Hankuk University of Foreign Studies; in Thailand, Princeton-in-Asia fellows went to work at Assumption University, Bangkok Christian College, Chiang Mai University and Payap University.

CAREERS IN ASIA

By the time the '80s rolled around, Princeton-in-Asia was increasingly aware that it was serving as a catalyst for young people who eventually developed careers in Asia or with Asian ties. But Princeton-in-Asia was always more matrimonial agency than employment agency; it introduced Asia to young people, many of whom fell in love with it.

The Asian economic miracle was in full bloom and American firms were expanding rapidly in that part of the world. After completing their assignments, many Princeton-in-Asia fellows went back to the States for advanced degrees and/or some job training and then returned to Asia, sent by employers who wanted to make use of their Asia backgrounds. Princeton-in-Asia alumni were prominent throughout Asia in

*T*HE TIGERS *in the picnic scene to the left are Indian. They are in a carving on a temple door and depict the Hindu god Shiva with his family and various animals. The meaning of the character is "friend."*

business, banking, law, and journalism. In 1987 Hamilton Meserve '59, President of Princeton-in-Asia, was quoted in the Princeton Alumni Weekly on how Princeton-in-Asia was playing an important role in international business. "The corporate world is beginning to sense, mainly in Japan, but also in Korea and Taiwan, that if it is going to survive into the 21st century economically, it is going to have to not only participate internationally in the world economy, it is going to have to become international." Today, 60% of the Princetonians working in Asia started their careers with Princeton-in-Asia.

The second big change was China, where the number of fellowships grew rapidly in the late '80s. Barney Williamson, who had spent more than a decade as a business executive in Asia before his retirement in 1985, had many contacts in China. He enlisted their help and that of the growing number of Princeton alumni with China connections to establish numerous new teaching positions.

A number of the new jobs were at colleges and universities in cities far from the metropolises of Beijing or Shanghai or Guangzhou, the three cities

*C*HRISTINE KUAN (Rutgers '96), an intern at Beijing University, meets Ye Dao-Chun and Sun You-Yun, two former students of Princetonians at Yenching University in the late 1930s. Yenching was renamed Beijing University in 1952. Next to the women is a monument to Randolph Sailer '19, who taught at Yenching for nearly two decades. A journal that Ms. Ye and Ms. Sun presented P-i-A has this to say about Sailer: "In and out of class he treated students as equals and friends, encouraging free discussion and problem solving on students' part rather than feeding them with ready answers."

where the majority of foreigners lived. Princeton-in-Asia fellows were among the few Americans living in such places as the northern port of Dalian and central province of Hubei. One such place was Wuhan, a city that Lyric Wallwork Winik '88 remembers as a "rough, gritty place with cholera outbreaks and hepatitis scares." "Back then, foreigners stood out in Wuhan," Lyric says. "I could not leave my apartment without children pointing at me and crying, *'waiguo ren, waiguo ren'* ('foreigner, foreigner')."

Princeton-in-Asia fellows in China sometimes were in the news themselves. Julia Sensenbrenner '83, a teacher at Fudan University in Shanghai, remembers President Reagan's visit there in 1984, when U.S. TV crews interviewed Princeton-in-Asia fellows and shot footage of how they lived. A few Princeton-in-Asia fellows even made it into the movies, moonlighting in the 1987 film "The Last Emperor." Back at home, during the '80s Princeton-in-Asia sponsored several seminars on Chinese business and politics both at the university and in Washington, D.C.

TIANANMEN SQUARE INCIDENT

And then Tiananmen Square happened. On June 4, 1989 the Chinese government's suppression of pro-democracy demonstrations in Beijing captured world headlines—and Princeton-in-Asia's phone in Palmer Hall started ringing off the hook as

'Tiananmen' in Wuhan

By Lyric Wallwork Winik '88
Princeton-in-Asia (China)

I first heard about what would become Tiananmen Square on a train, after a day trip with my students. It was mid-April, long before the name "Tiananmen Square" was emblazoned in the international lexicon. My student, Joshua, told me. He was nearly 40 then and an English teacher from a rural Hubei Province town. Sitting on the hard wooden seats that came with a third class train ticket, he said, "Hu Yaobang has died. Did you know Hu Yaobang? He was a great leader for the Chinese people." At the time, the comment meant nothing. Only later would I grasp its daring—only when I saw Joshua on the streets of Wuhan, marching. And too, I did not know Hu Yaobang, the former communist party secretary and supporter of political rights, whose death sparked Tiananmen.

That evening, we returned quietly to Hubei College of Education in Wuhan, a cramped, concrete place of rubble piles and rats that roamed the pipes, in the shadow of the famous Yellow Crane tower and the eight-lane bridge that traversed the Yangtze, at the spot where Mao supposedly swam the river. That afternoon, Wuhan had seen its first demonstration. Come Saturday and Hu Yaobang's funeral, thousands of students jammed the streets again, waving banners that said: "Freedom," "Democracy," and "Down With Dictatorship." But afterwards, an uneasy quiet enveloped everything. From Beijing, there were reports of student sit-ins and police beatings. And in Wuhan, we watched and waited, until mid-May, when ground zero reached my campus and my classroom.

On May 16, students from Wuhan's 30 colleges and universities began marching. They hoisted homemade flags and banners tied to freshly cut tree branches. And they were euphoric, convulsed in a tide of hope and optimism. The air crackled with the promise of change. There was joy everywhere, completely unrestrained. A Chinese colleague described it as the release of "so many emotions buried for so very long."

The marchers' ultimate destination was the vast Yangtze River bridge. That May and into June, the bridge became Wuhan's Tiananmen. From May 16 until the morning of May 21, thousands of protesters controlled the span, each day growing more emboldened. Some commandeered trucks and buses to reach the structure, but most walked the five or more miles from their dorms. Crowds applauded as they passed. Old woman handed out tea. Supporters carried food, drinks, cigarettes, and money. I watched them all. The bridge was around the corner from Hubei College of Education.

At first, that bridge was like a festival. Students and workers, the educated and the barely literate, converged. Women nursed babies. Old men leaned on sticks. Children scampered. But there was a powerful political

side. Crowds encircled student speakers. Banners attacked China's leader Deng Xiaoping and his deputy, Li Peng. Rumors flew that Deng had sought safety in Wuhan. My students cried, "Down with Deng Xiaoping." But youthful chants and banners would ultimately be no match for tanks and guns. At 12:01 a.m. on May 20, the euphoria turned. Martial law was declared in Beijing. In Wuhan, students took to the streets, angrily chanting and defiantly beating a large drum. Soon, my college gate was locked. I was left in my apartment, my supply of propane for boiling water dwindling. With only the anxious broadcasts of the Voice of America radio reporter in Beijing, I felt like a prisoner, wandering among my three small rooms.

Tuesday, May 23, 40,000 iron and steel workers joined the Wuhan students and struck for two days. Once again, everyone headed for the bridge. I watched them pass, feeling my veins course with adrenaline. That afternoon, police arrested 20 demonstrators and beat 200 others. Seizing buses, students and workers rushed to "counter the vio-

lence." For two days, bridge traffic stopped, but not time. Inside my apartment, my propane supply was gone. I could not boil water to drink. I had no way to cook, nothing to eat but a jar of peanut butter and some cookies. And I had nowhere to go. People retreated behind concrete walls. The college resembled a ghost town. Among the students too, energy was draining. They seemed tired, apprehensive, drawn. "Democracy" was like gossamer to them, a fragile thread, hard to grasp and build upon.

Then slowly the streets cleared, and city buses resumed their runs. A precarious normalcy crept back into Wuhan. But on Saturday June 3, we heard reports of troop movements and tear gas in Beijing. The next morning, I awoke to the pounding of the drum. As news of the Tiananmen massacre spread, Wuhan erupted. Tens of thousands marched to the bridge, chanting "Hang Li Peng, Death to Li Peng." Grim-faced crowds lined the streets. Some were weeping. That afternoon, thousands lay on the train tracks, paralyzing the Beijing-Guangzhou train line. Afraid of violence, the protesters left at dusk, as police moved in. But come daylight, the police vanished, and protesters returned to block the traffic and trains. Around the city, lamps and walls were splattered with red paint, signifying blood. I bicycled past them and along roads barricaded with disabled buses, their tires slashed and windows shattered. People began to hoard food. I started to give away my clothes, my books, all my things. "Go," friends and students told me. But I felt like a coward for fleeing.

Demonstrations continued, and, on June 7, the People's Liberation Army surrounded Wuhan. Black smoke billowed as city buses burned, and soldiers took control of the bridge. They were young men, with ill-fitting uniforms and unwieldy guns. But they smiled on their transport trucks, cold smiles, suggesting that they were cocky and capable of anything. At dusk, protesters marched through the campuses, imploring people to prevent the army from entering. It was the last march I saw. At dawn, I rode to the airport, past burning shops. Hours later, I left for Guangzhou. Below me, the city teetered between chaos and crackdown.

Later, safe in Hong Kong, I learned there had been no Wuhan massacre. Crackdown had prevailed. Only dreams died there that June. 🐎

calls from frantic parents came pouring in. By then Princeton-in-Asia had 43 fellows in China, scattered throughout the country. The Board, after consultation with the U.S. Embassy, Princetonians in China, and the University's experts on China, decided to order the fellows to leave China immediately. This was more easily said than done because most of the fellows lived in dorms or campus apartments and were difficult, if not impossible, to reach by phone or fax. "We were on the phone to China constantly, trying to figure out what was going on and where our people were," Barney later told the Princeton Alumni Weekly. Rob Pease '83, a former Princeton-in-Asia fellow and soon-to-be Executive Director, was back in Princeton, helping Barney with the calls to China. One harrowing call was to a fellow holed up at the Jianguo Hotel in Beijing, where Rob could hear the sound of gunfire in the distance.

Not until 10 days after June 4 were all the fellows who wanted to leave the country evacuated. (Rob remembers a Romeo and Juliet who were reluctant to depart because they were secretly engaged to be married and didn't want their parents to know.) Most ended up in Hong Kong, where local Princetonians set up a receiving station, meeting them at the airport or train, finding accommodation, and making sure they managed to sort out air tickets home. John Kamm '72 was one of the organizers and Hong Kong tycoon Gordon Wu '58 footed a large hotel bill, Barney recalls.

P-I-A INTERNS *learn that street life in Asia can be far richer in possibilities than life along Nassau Street. Yet the crowds, the noise and the constant activity can be a jolt. "The day after I arrived in Tokyo in the fall of 1987, I called my parents from a pay phone on the street, wailing that I'd made the wrong decision," remembers Susan Kirr '86. "I was completely overwhelmed by the confusion, the culture, the language, the transportation system, the shock of it all!" Here, some card players attract the attention of a crowd in Wuhan, China, and the camera of Lyric Wallwork Winik '88.*

Once the safety of the fellows had been ensured, Princeton-in-Asia faced another challenge: how to determine its future in China. Just as the Princeton-Yenching Foundation had been slow to leave China in 1949, mindful of its responsibilities to students there, Princeton-in-Asia was reluctant to abandon its program in China post-Tiananmen. Forty-four students had already been selected to fill positions in China in 1989-90. Was it safe for them to go? Was it fair to abandon the institutions that had been promised teachers?

In the end, the Board decided to cut the number of 1989-90 China fellowships to 11 and to limit them to the cities of Dalian and Guangzhou. Both cities had good communications facilities and international airports, which would be helpful in the case of further political upheaval. Unlike Beijing and Wuhan, which had been centers of political protest, neither Dalian nor Guangzhou had experienced much student unrest.

In addition, before they left Princeton, the 11 new fellows went through an intensive three-day briefing, in which returned fellows discussed their experiences in China and warned the new batch about avoiding overt political activity and not implicating Chinese students or colleagues.

MORE FORMAL STRUCTURE

The Tiananmen experience changed Princeton-in-Asia in a fundamental way. It "was the catalyst for formalizing the internships and making sure the office knew where the interns were and how they were doing," says Margaret Hazlett '88, a former fellow in Thailand and Japan and Executive Director from 1992-94.

This shift, accomplished over several years, manifested itself in several ways. First, the program was permanently cut back to 75-80 positions so that the office could devote more attention to each young person abroad. Somewhere about this time, the "fellows" started being called "interns." In 1995, with the assistance of Richard Eu '44 and former intern Jon Wonnell '81, Princeton-in-Asia opened a field office in Singapore. Located on the campus of Ngee Ann Polytechnic, the field office helps Princeton-in-Asia communicate more easily with the growing number of interns and host institutions in Southeast Asia.

Second, a formal, on-campus orientation was begun, thanks to a grant from the Henry Luce Foundation. Previous interns had been "oriented" by being handed a stack of intern reports from the country where they were headed and, if they were at Princeton, occasionally receiving a few classes on the rudiments of teaching English as a second language. But now, under Rob Pease's watch, a mandatory orientation program started in 1990, offering health tips, teacher training, basic language study, country-specific data, and a general discussion on the ethics of living abroad. The orientation program has since been expanded and continues today, with all the would-be interns brought together on the Princeton campus for several days in May. In addition, Margaret Hazlett started an on-campus re-entry and debriefing program with an emphasis on career options for returning interns.

Third, Princeton-in-Asia took steps to prepare for future emergencies. It bought evacuation insurance, gave interns international phone cards and the names of local contacts, and required all interns to sign a contract promising, among other things, to leave the country if so advised by the home office. As Barney puts it, "We came to realize that if we sent interns abroad without the infrastructure to support them, we were taking big risks." By the mid-1990s, nearly every intern, even in the remotest locations, was on e-mail.

By the early 1990s, Princeton-in-Asia had become the biggest employer of Princeton's senior class, as it is today, with about 5% of graduating seniors going off to work in Asia on internships. A 1990 ad in the Daily Princetonian asks: "What kind of placement service talks Princeton seniors into hard work at low pay in locations thousands of miles from home?"

Adventures can also bring dangers, as Margaret Crotty '94 found out as an intern in Indonesia. Margaret, a fellow at Save the Children in Jakarta, drew interna-

LUKE DAVIS '95 an intern at Shue Yan College in Hong Kong, accepts the booby prize (a college coffee mug) in the annual faculty-student basketball game. Below, Luke takes a break in Yunnan Province, China. The man with the bike, Luke remembers, was a friendly local who chased him and Sara Keckler '94 until they agreed to go out to a nearby lake and watch the cormorants fishing.

tional notice for her bravery in 1996, when she handed out life preservers to fellow passengers on a sinking ferry off the coast of Sumatra. Margaret, who was without a life preserver herself, was one of only 47 survivors of the 385 passengers on board. In May 1998, as anti-government demonstrations turned violent on college campuses in Indonesia, Princeton-in-Asia ordered its six interns there to leave.

NEW PLACEMENTS AND NEW COUNTRIES

The 1990s have seen the expansion of the program in several important ways. One is the creation of positions at several humanitarian organizations such as Save the Children and PLAN International, jobs that usually go to interns who have already served one year as teachers. Another is the evolution of the teaching jobs. "As many Asian countries have developed, we have broadened our scope to meet their changing educational needs," says Carrie Gordon, Executive Director since 1994. "For example when Singapore's labor force needs changed, we responded by sending instructors in engineering, computer science and biotechnology, rather than English. Japanese universities no longer need scores of English teachers, but we found that our interns' skills are in demand by Japanese companies, local governmental offices and secondary schools."

S ETH GROSSMAN '94 (center) and Eric Peng '94 teach a class at Peizheng Middle School in Guangzhou, China. Peizheng is the alma mater of Clyde Wu, who, with his wife Helen, sponsors P-i-A internships there and elsewhere in China.

In addition, Princeton-in-Asia has expanded to three countries that had been off-limits to Americans until very recently: Vietnam, Laos and Kazakhstan. These countries are too poor to provide even the most basic of stipends for foreign teachers and so Princeton-in-Asia, which otherwise could not afford to send interns there, sought outside help. In Vietnam and Laos, the fellows are supported by the Princeton University Class of 1969 and in Kazakhstan they were supported first by the Agency for International Development (AID) and now by U.S. oil companies with offices there. The annual cost of a position is between $3,000 and $7,000.

The story of how Princeton-in-Asia got into Kazakhstan is a classic example of how the program establishes new internships–through a serendipitous blend of hard work and good timing. In 1992, Stephen Robb '90, an intern in Korea, accompanied a Korean professor to Almaty, where they helped establish a business school, the first of its kind in this new country. Hearing about Steve's trip, Carrie enlisted the help of Margaret Osius '77, a former Princeton-in-Asia intern in Japan whose consulting job took her frequently to Kazakhstan. Meg visited the school, negotiated the internships, and then took it upon herself to find funding for them.

As the memory of Tiananmen Square faded, a number of new positions opened in China in the 1990s, several due to the generosity of Dr. Clyde Wu and his wife

LIFE IN THE WILD WEST

Blair Blackwell '96 visits Khiva, Uzbekistan in 1996. It's a long ride home to Almaty.

BY BLAIR BLACKWELL '96
PRINCETON-IN-ASIA (KAZAKHSTAN)

Upon telling friends and acquaintances that I was moving to Kazakhstan after graduation from Princeton in 1996, most asked what "that" was. Many didn't even realize such a country existed.

Situated in the heart of post-Soviet Central Asia, Kazakhstan is bigger than Western Europe and a land of contradictions and extremes. It is freezing in the winter and boiling in the summer. It is a land of vast wealth for some and great poverty for the majority.

Those who know Central Asia often compare it to the Wild West. Fabulously wealthy businessmen will shut down whole restaurants for their personal use and armed body guards patrol the ski slopes. I've grown accustomed to walking past several Mercedes and through a metal detector to get into a disco. The disco may be exclusive but that doesn't mean that it is palatial or even attractive. Rather, it will often be in a run-down old building where there is no heat downstairs and a tattered babushka (pensioner) takes your coat.

I live in the city of Almaty, once known as Alma Alta and until recently the capital of the country. Even the physical make-up of the city contradicts itself. What man made in Almaty is hideously bland; pollution often envelops the identical cement block buildings. Yet, the natural beauty of the mountains is one of the main reasons I stay. Snow-capped mountains, crystal blue lakes, and beautiful valleys beckon every weekend. It is a cleansing both of the lungs and the soul.

Princeton-in-Asia started in Kazakhstan in 1993 and we are still looking for the perfect niche at the Kazakhstan Institute of Management, Economics and Strategic Research or KIMEP. KIMEP is a graduate institute created to teach Western business management and public policy in English, the international language of business. Ironically, this school that teaches capitalism is housed in the building that once was home to the High Communist Party School—and where a few diehard Communists still wander the halls.

My year as a Princeton-in-Asia intern wasn't easy but it was worthwhile and enriching. I learned to live with the frustration of the leftover Communist redtape; for example, it took a month of fighting the bureacracy just to receive a supply of envelopes. Princeton-in-Asia interns have worked odd jobs at KIMEP, never truly understanding precisely where we fit in but always managing to find something useful to do. I worked in public relations, fundraising and administration. One of my predecessors was the school's job placement officer. And in spite of the difficulties, Princeton-in-Asia has contributed to the educational and economic development of KIMEP.

Some days are sheer excitement. There was the time that the entire city moved outside because a psychic in Moscow had predicted an earthquake; the teacher in the office across from mine ran me out of the building. Or the time I went skiing at a local slope but found the bus ride home much more exciting, as we did 360s all the way down the mountain.

Other days, however, are sheer boredom and I'm filled with frustration that I can't find stimulating conversation, go to a decent restaurant, a museum, a show or even a bookstore. I lament that life here is not colorful or vibrant, but often dull gray, like the streets.

Two of us have been bitten by the Central Asian bug and remained here in Almaty to work for multinational firms. Now, as a tax and legal services consultant for Price Waterhouse, I am continuing to take part in the economic and business reform that is such a key part of the nation's future. Even though I have graduated from intern to businesswoman, I hasten to note that the frustrations of dealing with bureaucracies and complications have not diminished.

Living in a country in transition from communism to capitalism is both exciting and challenging; I feel that I'm a part of history in the making. I witness daily what I spent four years in the basement of East Pyne seeking to understand, as I struggled with my senior thesis on the law in Russia.

The longer I am here, the more I realize that I need to learn and the more I appreciate the process of understanding. I constantly struggle to make sense of it all. I realize that this could be said of so many things in life. And I also realize that what you make of life depends on the eyes through which you look. I'm grateful to Princeton-in-Asia for making my own eyes sharper. 🐎

SCOTT DAVIS '89, then Program Director of P-i-A, pays a field visit to Indonesia in 1992, where he is pictured in a rice field north of Yogyakarta. Like all of P-i-A's program directors, Scott is a former intern (Indonesia). All of the managers of P-i-A's field office in Singapore have also been from the program, though there the job is actually an internship, where the intern divides his time between teaching and running the office.

CHRIS KIM '95 (opposite page, top) takes a break from his internship at Kyongyu Junior College in South Korea (now Sorabol College) to try to attract the attention of the gods at a Buddhist temple.

MARI FUKUDA GROVER '95 (opposite page, bottom) cozies up to two nio, or temple guards, whose job it is to scare evil spirits away from a shrine in Miyajima, Japan. Mari spent a summer as an intern at Kajima Corp. in Tokyo and then went on to work in Osaka for a company called Rock Paint. When it came time for her to leave, she persuaded her bosses to turn the job into a P-i-A internship.

K ENJA HASSAN '94 (left) and Megan Katz
'96 take a meditation class in Chiang
Mai, Thailand.

How Do You Say 'Immersion' in Mandarin?

BY CRAIG STUART '92
PRINCETON-IN-ASIA (THAILAND)

Princeton in Beijing sounds like a straight-forward derivative of its sponsor, and indeed the program fits neatly within Princeton-in-Asia's broader mission of building bridges between East and West. Far from being a supporting player, though, Princeton in Beijing has an entirely distinct goal of intensive language instruction; almost from its inception it has been considered the premier summer program of its kind.

"People come out of it either irritated with the amount of work they had to do, or really pleased with how much Chinese they learned," says Victoria Su, program coordinator in 1997. Either way, no one mistakes the summer for a lightweight cultural experience.

Princeton in Beijing tries hard to make sure students expect this. It emphasizes that the program covers an entire academic year's worth of study in eight weeks, suggesting that sightseeing be done before or after the program. Students are nonetheless adept at squeezing in what they can, either taking day trips on the weekends or, as one group did in 1997, flying to Mongolia for the three-day weekend that breaks up the program's two semesters.

There is no doubt that the Beijing location adds a cultural experience, with students learning as much about China as they do about the Chinese language. Conversations about democracy have been inevitable, particularly in 1997 when the handover of Hong Kong offered an immediate context for discussions on China's future. Whatever the topic, the conversation must be in Mandarin since all but the first-year students must pledge to speak only Chinese for the duration of the program. If this seems tough, it works.

The idea for Princeton in Beijing originated with Professor Chih-ping Chou, director of Princeton University's Chinese Language Program and for many years head of the highly regarded summer language program at Middlebury College in Vermont. The instruction techniques Professor Chou developed, which include tough drill routines and a strict attention to tones, are considered hallmarks of the program's success.

When Professor Chou stepped down as

The first Princeton in Beijing brochure.

director of the Middlebury program in 1992 he decided he wanted to create an even better program in China. Perry Link, a fellow professor in Princeton's East Asian Studies Department, whose help Professor Chou recruited at the outset, was skeptical. This was just three years after Tiananmen Square, and Professor Link was unsure whether the Chinese government would agree to a program that would bring in an American director, American teachers and American books. "I just didn't think it would work, politically or bureaucratically," he said.

But Professor Chou persevered. Instead of seeking contacts in the central government, which he believed would be counterproductive, he went directly to universities in several cities, including Beijing, Harbin and Kunming. The response was almost uniformly enthusiastic, and political concerns proved minimal. A language program was considered relatively benign and hosting American students was seen as a way to improve China's image in the West. When Professor Chou settled on Beijing Normal University, the trickiest part of the arrange-

ment was the financial terms.

Establishing the program on the American end was more difficult. Funding was not the issue; Professor Chou found pitching the idea to the Luce Foundation, with its interest in Asia and familiarity with the Middlebury program, "like preaching to the converted." But the new language program needed a sponsoring organization and the obvious choice, Princeton University, had a standing practice of not running overseas programs. And so Princeton-in-Asia agreed to be the sponsor.

The program, envisioned for 35 to 40 students, has grown quickly. Interest was so high that 86 students attended in the first year. By 1997 the program had expanded to 130 students. Six American teachers and about 25 hired in China ensured a student-faculty ratio of four-to-one.

The program has not been problem-free. BNU's dingy dorms, with their communal, squat toilets, have drawn criticism from students. More substantively, in the spring of 1996, Professor Chou was informed that he should revise certain passages of a book he used. One offending passage had youths discussing contraception (a topic of practical value for its ability to get the PiB students talking in the classroom) without specifying that these were American and not Chinese youths. Professor Chou felt it important to avoid the appearance of editing the book according to specific requests. So instead of making the requested changes he decided to produce a new book, which he wrote in a matter of weeks before departing for Beijing at the start of the summer.

Most troubling of all has been Perry Link's visa problems. Upon arriving at the Beijing airport in 1996, Professor Link was denied entrance. He suspects this was due to commentary he gave on the Chinese-language services of the BBC and Voice of America, in which, he says, he did not deliberately attempt to be provocative but spoke his mind freely on such issues as the treatment of dissidents in China.

In an increasingly crowded field of summer language programs in China, Princeton in Beijing stands out and is running strong.

In 1995 Princeton University assumed responsibility for academic oversight and began giving university course credit through the registrar's office. Graduates of Princeton in Beijing are considered an appealing China-tested pool of candidates for Princeton-in-Asia positions, and have proven adept at taking on the responsibilities of Princeton-in-Asia's teaching internships in China. 🐾

Helen; their son, Roger, is a member of the Princeton Class of 1986. "Our lives have been straddled between two cultures, namely Chinese and American," says Clyde, in explaining why he and Helen decided to sponsor the Princeton-in-Asia internships. "It is always our desire to contribute whatever we can to promote cultural understanding and awareness between these two cultures." The Wus fund internships at Peizheng Middle School, Clyde's alma mater in Guangzhou Province; Peking Union Medical College; and Beijing University.

"We stress to the interns that by their own examples and way of life, they will demonstrate to their Chinese counterparts what America is," says Clyde. "In return, through their people-to-people contact, the Princeton-in-Asia interns will bring back with them an understanding of the real Chinese culture and experience." There is no better summary of what Princeton-in-Asia is all about.

Atsushi Fukushima, vice president of NEC Logistics in Tokyo, explains why his company sponsors Princeton-in-Asia

SUSAN KIRR '86 (left) and Tracy Roberts '87 held internships at the Japan Times, thanks to the generosity of Toshiaki Ogasawara, publisher of the English-language daily.

interns: "In the long term, we expect our involvement to engender better Pan-Pacific relations. In recent years there have been between 40,000 and 50,000 Japanese students studying in the U.S. In Japan, the number of American students is only about 3,000. Please note that this is substantially worse than the trade deficit. This imbalance leads to misunderstanding between our two nations but it can be avoided if there is a greater interchange of ideas. Although our role in providing a solution to this problem is small, the roots of our efforts are spreading and it is quite possible that in the future, those interns may play a major role between their mother countries and Japan."

The 1990s also saw the startup of Princeton in Beijing, one of Princeton-in-Asia's most notable achievements. In 1993 Professors Chih-ping Chou and Perry Link established an intensive Chinese-language training program at Beijing Normal University. Princeton in Beijing quickly became the premier Chinese-language school for American university students, teaching more than 100 students every summer.

Carrie Gordon calls Princeton-in-Asia a "miracle program." In its Centennial year of 1998-99, it is sending 82 interns to 10 countries on a budget of $150,000. The money comes from its endowment (40%), individuals (25%), foundations (23%) and application fees (12%). Some 60% of the interns are from Princeton University.

SECOND CENTURY CAMPAIGN

In 1998, at the beginning of the Centennial year, the Board of Trustees approved a plan for Princeton-in-Asia's second century and launched its first major capital campaign, under the chairmanship of John Langlois '64 and Ruth Stevens, Kirkland College '72, both Princeton-in-Asia alumni. The aim is to "secure the future of the

A VIETNAMESE TYPHOON

BY SCHUYLER ROACH '96
PRINCETON-IN-ASIA (VIETNAM)

The slow, dreamy peasant life glorified in Oliver Stone's movie serves better to illustrate what Vietnam is not than what it is. From my first harrowing car ride from the airport to Hanoi in September 1997, my life in Vietnam has been a typhoon-esque whirlwind of action, emotion, joy, frustration and constant awe.

I landed in Hanoi on a Wednesday night, had my first day of work at Save the Children on Friday, and was off to the field to see the nutrition projects by Sunday. In the course of my first six weeks I made five or six more field visits to observe various international non-government organizations' programs and was given a microfinance/nutrition project to manage.

Save the Children began working in Vietnam in 1990 on a poverty alleviation and nutrition project that has successfully rehabilitated tens of thousands of children, relying only on local resources. Recently we began work on a project to combine nutrition with small, short-term loans to poor women in an effort to increase incomes and expand the impact of established programs. I arrived just in time to manage this new program. I

couldn't have been busier...or happier. During those first six weeks I fell in love with this place and haven't recovered.

As you drive to the villages on the tree-lined, elevated roads between the rice paddies, it feels as though you are driving to an island in a sea of green. If you were to step out of the car there is no doubt you would splash into the depths. When I first arrived, it was harvest time in north Vietnam. The country roads were paved with golden hay, and people stayed outside working together from sunrise to sunset. Buffaloes munched on mounds of dried rice stalks, the corners of every house disappeared under piles of yellow-husked rice, and the feeling of plenty was contagious.

Thanh Hoa Province, where Save the Children works, is extremely poor yet well kept. The brown and gold mud huts are sparse and sleek with delicate flashes of pink and purple from the carefully tended flowering vines draped over the gates. Families live in one room and have only minimal furnishings, which include beautifully carved antique beds, an occasional table or chair that would probably fetch thousands at Sotheby's, and, inevitably, a bamboo pipe for the men to smoke local grasses.

The dedicated and capable women I work with speak painfully slow Vietnamese with me—the only Vietnamese I can understand—and constantly admire my strength and

height. *"Beo lam,"* (meaning very big) they remark with approval, unable to see how that might be considered an insult. I can't either, having seen the malnutrition that affects 26% of children in rural Vietnam. Yet, in spite of the gravity of the problems these women face and the chronic need for development programs, most of the trips I make to rural areas have a festive air about them. The children gawk and the women giggle wherever I go.

During one meeting before an audience of about a hundred women, I made the mistake of asking them if they had any questions for me. After the usual how old are you, are you married, how long have you been in Vietnam, they asked me to sing. Trying to escape, I insisted that someone else sing first. One stunning young woman was only too happy to sing a beautiful traditional song, leaving me in the even more uncomfortable position of following her act. I opted to invite the bravest of the crowd of children who had gathered to stare to join me in the hand motions to "You Are My Sunshine." The Vietnamese gave my feeble attempt a most gracious reception.

The amazing thing about being in Vietnam is that in the short time I've been here nothing has slowed down, and every day brings a new adventure. I couldn't tell you what will happen tomorrow if I tried. Princeton-in-Asia has given me more than a life-changing experience; it's given me a life-defining experience. 🐎

organization," says David Newberg '76, President. The money raised in the Second Century Campaign will go to three broad areas: grants for travel and language study for selected interns on an as-needed basis; more in-field support; and Princeton-in-Asia's highest priority, new internships in the poorest countries of Asia.

"Each year Princeton-in-Asia receives requests for teachers and international development volunteers to work in developing countries in Indochina, Central Asia and the less developed regions of China and Nepal," says Carrie. "Unfortunately, many of these prospective host institutions are unable to fully fund such positions. But the chance to help develop the educational resources of these countries is true to Princeton-in-Asia's original pioneering vision."

INTERNS OF THE 1990s

What kind of young man or woman becomes a Princeton-in-Asia fellow today? Carrie sees two general types of applicants. "One group is students who have studied Asian languages or politics or history. A P-i-A internship is a logical step for them to jumpstart an Asian career." The other pool of interns is something entirely different, she says. "These are students who want to get off that treadmill, look around them and see what the world has to offer. A lot of these students are med school or law school bound."

In addition, the 1990s have seen a number of Princeton students of Asian heritage in the Princeton-in-Asia program—Chinese-Americans, Japanese-Americans, Korean-Americans, Vietnamese-Americans. "There are definitely some students with very personal reasons for wanting to go to Asia," Carrie says. One example is Chen Haiyin '98, an electrical engineer who was born in Beijing. Haiyun, who has been selected for the 1998-99 program, is planning to teach engineering in Singapore because she wants to observe another Chinese society at close hand. Joe Nguyen '93, a refugee from Vietnam, had an internship in Singapore and stayed on to work there. Ng Chiang-ling '96, a Singaporean, was an intern at NEC Logistics in Japan from 1996-98. In a few such cases, Carrie points out, Princeton-in-Asia is now "building bridges between Asian nations" not just between the U.S. and Asia.

One hundred years later, Pop Gailey, Princeton-in-Asia's first "intern," can speak for the more than 1,200 young men and women who have followed him to Asia under the auspices of the Princeton Work, Princeton-in-Peking, the Princeton-Yenching Foundation and Princeton-in-Asia: "It is a privilege of the ages to be given the opportunity to live in such a time and to be in the atmosphere of such rapid and radical changes that go on before our very eyes."

Like Gailey, most of the Princeton-in-Asia interns have been teachers. But like Gailey, they have all learned more than they taught. Helping young men and women to see with their "very eyes" the riches of a culture and a people different from their own is what Princeton-in-Asia is all about.

EXECUTIVE DIRECTORS, pictured left to right on the opposite page, top row: Jason Eyster '74 (1983-85) Barney Williamson '43 (1985-89), Rob Pease '83 (1989-92). Bottom row: Margaret Hazlett '88 (1992-94) and Carrie Gordon (1994-present).

PRINCETON-IN-ASIA
A Century of Service
1898 - 1998

AFGHANISTAN
David Edwards
S. Peter Poullada

CHINA
Zachary Abuza
Laurence Alberts
Alexis Albion
Robert Allen
Stuart Allen
Keith Alverson
Garrett Anderson
Joel Anderson
Cathleen Christie Arch
Barbara Armas
Lisa Aslanian
Helen Atkinson-Barnes
Ron Atley
Jonathan Augustine
Alice Ayres
Lee Vaughn Barker
Robert G. Barnes
Elizabeth Barr
Red Morris Barrett
David Basson
Diana Bauer
Mark Baughan
Alexander Beal
Stewart Becker
Sean Bell
Laura Benedict
Alison Bing
John Bischoff
Stacey Black
Edward Boland
Jill Bouma
Gardner Bovingdon
Mosemarie Boyd
Anthony Brasunas
Charlotte Brooks
Lynnley Browning
Katherine Brownlee
Kathryn Warren Buck
John Stewart Burgess
Katherine Burns
Laura Burt
David Cantalupo
Michelle Capobres

Timothy David Carini
Allen Carlson
Melissa Carlson
Mark Carpenter
Donald W. Carruthers
Laura Pilar Casa
J. Wheaton Chambers
Jennifer Chan
Calvin Chang
Martin Chang
Michael Chang
Adam Charnes
Helen Cheng
Wendy Cheung
Douglas Chia
Stanley Ching
William "Dusty" Clayton
Audra Cleaveland
John Cobau
Frayda Cohen
Shannon Conaty
Heather Cook
James Cossman
Sarah Councell
Roberto Cuca
Erin-Siobhain Currin
Mark Dallas
Monique Daniels
John Danis
Paula Davidson
William Dederer
Philippe de Pontet
David Dimcheff
Elizabeth Dix
Robert Dodds
Robert M. Duncan
Mark Dunn
Frank Andrew Dressler
Foster Rhea Dulles
Laurie Duthie
William J.B. Edgar Jr.
Nathaniel Edmonds
Dwight W. Edwards
Sarah Eichberg
Jennifer Eikren
Bruce Einhorn
Marcia Ellis
Sarah Lee Elson

Norman Eng
Judith Engler
Rachel Factor
Grace Fan
David Feit
John T. Find
David Fisher
Marc Fogel
Charles Forcey
Susan Fou
Kimberly Fox
Elizabeth Frank
Abigail Franklin
Scott Fraser
Lloyd A. Free
Sara Friedman
Ronit Friedman
Lewis D. Froelick
Isabella Furth
Robert Reed Gailey
Mary Gallagher
Jeffrey Galvin
Sidney D. Gamble
Anthony Geron
Brian Gibel
Diane Brow Gifford
Robert Glucksman
Jessica Godfrey
Rebecca Golbert
Ellen Goldberg
James Goniea
Heather Gordon
James Green
Lisa Greenbaum
Ingrid Greenberg
Lisa Greenberg
Elisabeth Grinspoon
Seth Grossman
Pam Groves
Robert Gunther
Leif Haase
Caitlin Halligan
Peter Hammond
Amy Hanser
Emily Hantman
Jonathan Hartsel
Fiona Havers
Gretchen Heefner

Lisa Kennedy Heller
Stephen Herschler
Jeffrey Hesser
Charles L. Heyniger
Amos N. Hoagland
Lisa Hoffman
Daniel Holmes
John Holzman
Lucille Hornby
Tia Horner
Lawrence D. Howell
Avis Hsieh
Jennifer Huang
Cecile Hudson
Edward Hughes
Dawn Hummel
Harold Hummel
Barbara Hund
Matthew Hurlock
Daniel Hwang
Scott Jalowayski
Andrew Jen
Mark Jerng
Margaret Emily Johnson
Manami Kamikawa
Eric Karchmer
Solomon Karmel
Deborah Karush
Mary Kelleher
Ron Keren
Suzanne King
Joel Kirkhart
Merritt Klarsch
Nicola Klearman
W. Arden Koontz
Charles Kooshian Jr.
Julian Ku
Christine Kuan
Stephen Landis
Dune Lawrence
Laura Lazarus
Brian Lee
Gena Lentz
Syau-Jyun Liang
Bradley Lindenbaum
Joshua Lippard
Judy Liu
Madeleine Loh

George W. Loos
Theodore Lorenz
Michael Mann
Adam Marks
Eric Mason
Robin Matross
David Maynard
Christopher McCarthy
John McGill
John McHugh
Andrew McKinnon
Thomas McNeill
Lawrence M. Mead
Randall Mechem
Kathrine Meyers
Penelope Mihalap
Andrew Miller
David Miller
John Milne
Steven Mines
Liane Moody
Benjamin Morgan
Kate Morgenroth
Jeremy Brill Moya
Ryan Munoz
Mina Muraki
Bruce Mygatt
Rebecca Nedostup
Deidre Nickerson
Vicki Noble
Katharine Noel
Jeffrey Noles
Daniel Nossa
Michael Ohliger
Kerry O'Neill
Daniel Oscar
Katy Palmer
Maureen Pao
Jason Patent
A. Brodie Paul
Eric Peng
Truman C. Penney
Steven Persky
Stanley L. Phraner
Kevin Platt
Leslie Plomondon
Jeffrey Plunkett
Elizabeth Poon

Michael Lee Popa
Elizabeth Portale
Eric Price
Robert Quinn
Benjamin Quintana
Surekha Raghavan
Johanna Ransmeier
Michael Ravich
Raoul Rayos
Andrew Regier
Sarah Remijan
Ali Reza
Van Dusen Rickert Jr.
Bryan Ristow
Richard H. Ritter
Schuyler Roach
Jorge Robert
Jeffrey Rosalsky
Paul Ross
Edward Ruthazer
Matthew Saal
Randolph Sailer
Chris Sanchirico
Jamie Schroeder
David Schuler
Jessica Schultz
Louis R. Schmertz Jr.
Alan Schwartz
Jeffrey Schweinfest
Lawrence M. Sears
Julia Sensenbrenner
Jack Settles Jr.
Lawrence D. Seymour
Matthew Shallbetter
Daniel Shapiro
David Shaw
Joanne Shen
Samuel M. Shoemaker
Emily Shortridge
David Sincox
Debra Smart
Hilary Smith
Kristofer Smith
Sarah Smith
Jason Snyder
Helen Song
Theodore Cuyler Speers
Sarah Stein
John Underwood Stephens
John David Stewart
Laura Strausfeld
Jennifer Su
Dax Swanson
Allen G. Swede
Lennig Sweet
Lester Szeto
Yunsian Tai
Dina Tamburrino
Lynette Tan
Matthew Taylor
Richard Tompson
Yoeh-Liang Tong

Tara Tranguch
Philip Trujillo
Maria Trunk
Aileen Tsui
David Turchetti
Arthur B. Tyler
Anita Ung
Tiffany Vandeweghe
Albertine Vibert
Marjorie Victor
Daniel Vittum III
Ruth von Goeler
Leigh Vorhies
Anhna Vuong
Edward Barry Wall
Alex Wang
Jennifer Wang
Adria Warren
Andrew Weaver
Zhuofang Wei
Jodi Weinstein
Franklin C. Wells
Alexander Williams
Jennifer Williams
Eleanor Williamson
Matthew Williamson
Kenneth Orr Wilson
Nicole Wilson
Carol Wingard
Lyric Wallwork Winik
Aaron Wolfson
Amy Wong
Judy Wong
Deborah Wood
Alexandra Woodford
Hilary Wyss
Meipu Yang
Grace Shou-en Yang
Michael Yap
Marcia Yee
Peter Yeh
Marian Young
Walter S. Young
Alison Yu
Angela Yuan
Aaron Zdawczyk

EGYPT

Carter Abel
Jenny Barends Spalding
Katherine Bennison
Sarah Bentley
Karen Boyle
Lori Duke
Charles Finnie
Nicholas Griffin
William Haynes
Tara Joseph
Roy Oppenheim
Frank Packard
Timothy Reif
Sadiq Reza

Jennifer Tower
Joseph Warren

GREECE

Thomas Beaton
Daniel Caner
Anne Demitrack
Jason Fish
Heather McKey
Gunther Peck
Elizabeth Pulling
N. Peter Rousseau Jr.
John Stokes
J. Bradley Swanson
Daphne Wysham

HONG KONG

Owen Alterman
James Barnhart
Ralph Beha
Glenn Berkey
William Berlind
David Berry
Cynthia Chiu
John Luke Davis
Ronald W. Davis
Alexandra de Campi
Katharine Dunn
Karen Tonneberger Edgley
Gladys Epting
Stuart Essig
Kathryn Hayward-MacFarlane
Stephen Huff
Hugh Hughes
Emily Johnson
John R. Johnston
John Kamm
Michael Kammerer
Karen Karp
Susan Keuffel
Jane Leifer
Christian Lown
Elizabeth Lu
John McCobb Jr.
Richard McDermott
Jeffrey Muir
Scott Murphy
Owen Nee Jr.
Thomas Pniewski
Jason Press
Lisa Roberts
Robert Rosenthal
Hilary Roxe
Lewis Rutherfurd
Neil Seltzer
Rebecca Sonkin
Thomas Stewart
Annie Su
Amanda Terry
Carol Wan
Elizabeth Wiedenmayer
Steven Zwanger

INDIA

Brendan Byrne Jr.
Daniel Ciporin
Dana Dreibelbis
Laura Kogan
Tamar Laddy
J. Michael Orszag
Katherine Randall
Nancy Rappaport
Elizabeth Vickers Saarel
Alex Schafir
Catherine Slemp
William Sloan
Sarah Van Cleve van Doren
Lynn Weston
Julia Whitfield

INDONESIA

Adam Aston
John Baughman
Karen Brooks
Nadav Caine
Anne Callard
Alexandra Carey
John Cock
Laura Cooley
Richard Cozine
Margaret Crotty
Brian James Daly
Jamie Davidson
William Scott Davis
Steve Diamond
Brooke Ditmore
Nicole Fanarjian
Aimee Mechem Feeley
Ted Fishman
Margit Galanter
Beth Gardiner
Amy Golden
Barry Gruber
Emily Guthrie
Christian Hauschildt
Robert Hay
Lynn Heller
Rebecca Joseph
Martin Kenny
Anne Koerckel
Ken Latour
Katherine Linebaugh
Clark Lombardi
Maura Malarcher
Bruce Manciagli
Steven Manning
Christopher Meserve
Paul Minault
Wesley Neal
Laurie Hartman Nesseth
Hans Nesseth
David Newhouse
Sara Newmann
Michael Northrop

Ellen Novey
Lindley Odell
Leslie Patrascioiu
Eliot Highet Patty
Lori Pellegrino
Eleanor Peters
Peter Darin Prozes
Kristen Rainey
Kathleen Regan
Brian Russo
Justine Sass
Joshua Scodel
Laura Sedlock
Jill Shanebrook
Claire Siverson
Shannon Slavin
Mark Slidell
Alice Stackpole
Patrick Supanc
Michael Taila
William Thomas IV
Derek Thurber
David Tomberlin
Jiway Tung
Susan Turner
Thomas Tuttle
Brian Vogt
Anastasia Vrachnos
Jonathan Watts
Jonathan Weiss
Eric Westendorf
Laura Wolf
Randall Wood
Anna Zeni-Russo

IRAN

Juanita Burch
Michael Colopy
James "Jason" Eyster
Lawrence Fox
Richard Goldman
Frederick Leist
Linda Morton
George Roudebush Jr.
Katherine Traeger
Michael Whalen

JAPAN

David Abrams
Hugh Aiken
Jay Alabaster
Amrana Ali
James Aliferis
Mark Ambrose
Margarita Andreu
Tami Drummond Anton
Susan McMurry Archer
Leigh Armstrong
David Baffa
Michael Bailey
Margaret Baker
Eileen Harvey Bakke

Debra Tarnapol Ballen
John Baniewicz
Julie Barton
Daryl Baskerville
Samuel Bays
Stephen Belgrad
John Bell IV
Elizabeth Bennett
Loren Bentley
Brian Berghuis
Richard Berry
Gavin Beske
Mark Blaxill
Lucy Swift Bowman
Nancy Broadbent
Charles Brodhead
Ralph Brown
Robert Browne
William Brown Jr.
Blaine Brownell
Laurie Killackey Buckley
Naran Burchinow
R. Alexander Burnett
Neil Cable
Daniel Calacci
T. Scott Callon
Gregory Caltabiano
Peter Campbell
J. Carlo Cannell
Margaret Cannella
William Cardell
Timothy Carr
Nicole Cattell
Stephanie Chang
Effie Chao
John Christensen
Sara Cicerone
Michael Colangelo
W. Bruce Comer III
Norman Delaney Cook
Steven Cousins
Ann-Sophie Cremers
Thomas Croonquist
Matthew J. Crowley
Kristin Cuilwik
John Curby Jr.
Kevin Cuskley
Michael Cusumano Jr.
Jenny Keane Dalton
Maria Dans
Lara Darden
Russell DaSilva
Aisha Davis
Jeffrey Davis
Kevin Davis
Stuart Davis
Virginia Davis
Stephen DeCosse
Janina de Guzman
Robert DeLorenzo
Wendy Deslauriers
Francesco di Valmarana

H. C. Charles Diao
David Dichek
Maria Dommerich
Larry Dougherty
Maura Dougherty
Carl Drummond
Linda Dunbar
Jeff Dunoff
Patrick Dwyer
Alfred Dyer
Elizabeth Earle
Nancy Easton
P. Noriko Eda
Ken Egusa
Daniel Elkes
Jonathan Stuart Epstein
Melissa Eugenio
Cyndie Feaster-Washington
Richard Feiner
Fabrizia Fiamma
Peter Fincke
Marco Fiorentino
David Fletcher
Denise Foley
Craig Forman
Mary Foster
John Fou
John Fox
Bliss Freytag
Laura Fried
James Frierson
Daniel Fuchs
Harald Fuess
Yuko Fukuda
Bruce Fullerton
David Galef
John Gelblum
Donald George
Bryce Giddens
Bruce Ginsberg
Ann Glenn
Ann Glusker
James Gollin
Marjorie Greene
Peter Greenhill
Radmila Grin
Mari Fukuda Grover
Nicole Guerrier
Ben Guill
John O. Haley
Sven Martin Hallerdt
Joshua Hammer
Eric Han
Robert Chang-kun Han
Christopher Handte
Thomas Hare
David Harrower
Andrew Haruyama
Carol Hasson
Charles Hatfield II
Mark Hatfield

Thomas Havens
Rosemarie Havranek
Naomi Hayashi
John Hayes
Robert Hazel
Peter Hegelbach
Stephanie Henning
William Henry Jr.
Trevor Hill
Phillip 'Cam' Hillstrom
Jonathan Hines
Adrian Hinman
Margaret Holdsworth
Jamie Hood
Bethanie Hooker
John Hoover
B. Andrew Hoover III
Brandon Hornbeck
Nicholas Howard
Judith Howland
Kai-Lin Hsu
Louisa Huband
Jackson Huddleston Jr.
Sayako Huddleston
Harry Hummer
Gordon Hunt
Susan Hurley
Kristin Ito
Lydia Itoi
Susan Jackson
Peter Jaeger
Delia Jampel
Gary Jenkins
Polly Jessen
Eric Johnson
Elizabeth Johnson
Lee Johnson
Richard Johnson
Jeffrey Jones
Laurie Kahn-Leavitt
Lisa Kanemoto
Carroll Kaneta
Florence Kao
David Karel
Raivo Karmas
William Katen-Narvell
Charisse Kiino
James Kilduff
Colin Kim
Jeanie Kim
Merrill Shepherd King
Melanie Kirkpatrick
Susan Kirr
Robert Knapp
Mei Kobayashi
David Korones
Edward Kortney
Bonnie Kortrey
Deborah Kuan
Dana Laird
Venkateshwar Lal
Beth Landau

Michael Landweber
Steven Lang
Peter Langenberg
Yvette Saeko Lanneaux
Brian Lavoie
Robert Law
Lee Adair Lawrence
David Lee
James Lee III
Tanya Lee
Peter Lees
Peter Lehmen
Robert Leibowitz
David Lemon
Sheila Leniart
Eve Lesser
Jean Letai
William Levine
George Lewis
Jonathan Lewis
Staughton Lewis
Nancy Lin
Jennifer Linker
Richard Linowes
Wade Lippman
Kin Lo
Louis Lopez
Ernest Lorimer
Paul Loughnane
Elizabeth Lowe
James Lugannani
John MacIntosh
James Maffezzoli
Grant Mahood
Manuel Maisog
Martin Mansfield Jr.
Dean Manson
Roya Mansouri
Karen Marsh
Ralph Marshall
Peter Mattersdorff
Thomas Matthias
Keith Mayer
Robert Mayer
Susan Mayer
Peter McCagg
John McClure
Frank McCoy
Deborah McCue
Brigid McDermott
E. Andrew McDermott III
Paul McDermott
Joseph McFarland
Lisa McGloin
Robert Stuart McIlroy
Robert McInturff
Christopher McMurray
Sarah Meacham
Alan Meltzer
Joan Menzer
Hamilton Meserve
Jack Meyerson

Daniel Michaels
Robert Mikos
Laurel Miller
Catherine McCartney Miller
Ann Misback
Susan Mlot
Russell Moench
Hilary Monihan
Charles Monk Jr.
Koren Moore
Michael Moore
Ken Moritsugu
Harold Morlan II
Susan Muenzer
Bern Martin Mulvey
Michael Murray
Anna Muzzy
Mark Natkin
Chiang-Ling Ng
Darlene Nichols
John Noden
David O'Brien
Richard Obermann
Jane Ohgami
Terasa Wickersty Orlando
Charles Osborn
Margaret Osius
Karena Ostrem
John Oxenham
John Park Jr.
Young Park
Virginia Parker
Pat Patterson
Robert Pease
Samuel Perkins
Thomas Peters
Boris Petersik
Abigail Peterson
Dirk Peterson
Andrew Plaks
Alissa Short Poincenot
Lucy Prager
Cherish Pratt
Christina Propst
Elizabeth Rankin
Robert Ransom
Y. Rupa Rao
Ronnie Raymond
Karen Regelman
Thomas R. Reid III
Tierney Boyd Remick
H. Lawrence Remmel
David Remnick
Mark Reudelhuber
Morton Rible
Hilary Richards
Peter Ridgway
Andrew Ripps
Elliot Robbins
Tracy Roberts
Gary Robins
Edward Rodden

Edward Rogers
Keith Rogers
Robert Rogers Jr.
Aimee Rogstad Guidera
Thomas Rohlen
Barbara Romer
Jennifer Romero
Amy Carrico Root
Douglas Roskos
Kendrick Royer
Anne Swinton Ruggles
William Russell Jr.
Jeffrey Samberg
Andrew Sattee
Michael Schechner
Amy Schneider
Steven Schoeffler
Elizabeth Schwartz
Margaret Schwartz
Aaron Segal
Colleen Shanahan
Bruce Shaw
Marc Shaw
Pamela Sherrid
David Sherry Jr.
Betticlare Irminger Shimada
Cynthia Shimoda-Ohata
Steven Silver
Peter Simpson
Andrew Sinwell
Michael Skorski
John Sloboda
Jonathan Small
Cordelia Smela
Steve Smela
Emily Smith
Ramsey Smith
Stephanie Smith
Gregory Sokoloff
Penny Soppas
Dennis Spates
Pat Shaw Sprague
Kevin Staley
Andrew Steinberg
Neal Steinberg
J. Peter Stern
Charles Stevens
Ruth Stevens
Jennifer Stewart
Mary Stone
Olivia Streatfeild
Grant Strine
Mary Strother
Dana Winingder Sulger
Tina Sung
Rebecca Syrett
Joy Tadaki
Anne Tergesen
Page Thompson
Joyce Thornhill
Emily McNairy Thornton
Thor Thors

Kumi Tucker
Carla Vaccaro
Rachel Van der Voort
John Van Horne
Richard Van Horne
Elise van Oss
John Vann
Anna Verdi
Daniel Von Kohorn
Anthony Wahl
Pat Neff Walker
Juliette Walker
Preston Walsh
Aidan Wasley
Alison Watson
William Watson
Bruce Weiner
William West
Brendan White
James White
Yolanda Simmons White
Henry Whiteside Jr.
Jeffrey Wieser
Katherine O'Leary Wilcox
Susan Wilkinson
Peter Willett
Tamasin Foote Wilson
Jesse Witten
Scott Wolfson
Cameron Wu
Julie Yeh
Ying Zhou

JORDAN
Helen White

KAZAKHSTAN
Omer Alper
Blair Blackwell
Edgar Chen
Diego de Acosta
Molly Graves
Peter Hand
Kevin Julius
William Samuel Patten
Jeremy Roller
Erik Sabot
Emily Van Buskirk

KOREA
Cori Allen
Christopher Binns
Kelly Bromfield
John Carr III
Sun-Young Chi
Diane Cho
Amy Choe
Elisabeth Choi
Erin Chung
Tarim Chung
Matthew Corcoran
Jeffrey Cymet

J. Anthony Downs
Elizabeth Cooper Doyle
David Evers
Keith Ferguson
Andrew Fetter
Mark Frazier
John Gerhart
Jonathan Goldman
Lisa Carpi Gorsch
Daniel Grabon
Sean Greene
Elizabeth Haase-Meyers
Sandra Harris
Joon-yeung Huh
Peter Hunter
David Jacobs
Karyn Johnson
Scott Karchmer
Christopher Kim
Jina Kim
Kenneth Kim
Nancy Kim
John Knightly
Mary Sweeney Koger
Beth Kwon
Daniel Lee
Hio Kyeng Lee
Barry Levinson
Janda Lukin
John Marcom Jr.
Marcia Maynard
Cindy McBennett
Katharine Moir
Carolyn Mosteller
Justin Murray
Margaret O'Connor
Robert Oppenheim
Anneliese Pak
Edward Park
Allison Keller Planting
Miriam Rhew
Shauna Rienks
Peter Rim
Stephen Robb
F. Halsey Rogers
Richard Rorvig
Aspen Russell
George Sachs
Julie Sade
Elizabeth Seay
John Seel
I. Douglas Sherman
Hyun Ja Shin
Leah Sieck
David Sternlieb
Steve Sun
Marcus Choi Tye
Sharon Volckhausen
Jon Wallenstrom
Jennifer Wasserstein
Kevin White
David Williamson

Elizabeth Yang
Dana Yoo
Ari Zweiman

KUWAIT
James Rutherfurd

LAOS
Lloyd Brown
Brett Dakin

LEBANON
Robert Deraney
David Ray
Terry Wrong

MACAU
Bruce Kennedy
Karen Klitzman
Blake Locklin
Adrianne Nagy
Randle Seymour
Julia Tang
Toni Thompson
Vera Trojan
Movien Yee

MALAYSIA
Sarah Duxbury
Cary Hollinshead
Kathleen MacNamara
Kerrie Mitchell

SINGAPORE
Sarah Albano
Francis Allen Jr.
Kelley Aveilhe
Louise Avila
Jeffrey Baer
Thomas Bailey
Anne Barnhill
Omri Beer
Rebecca Birnbaum
Hans-Marcus Bitter
Robert Bolling III
Najja Bracey
Elizabeth Brown
Glenn Bryce
Katherine Canning
Kenneth Chang
Haiyin Chen
David Dawson
Katherine Dolan
Jacqueline DuBois
Scott Duncan
Kevin Durkin
Tiffany Ericksen
Erin Flannery
Bethany Freeman
Cornelius Gildea
Allan Gray
Edward Gung

Liahona Gustafson
Marc Hadfield
Jesse Hammons
Alysia Han
Gregory Harding
Jeffrey Henderson
Kendra Hershey
Jessica Hittle
Isaac Ho
Jennifer Howlett
Pei-Lin Hsiung
Helen Hu
Matthew Janis
Sara Keckler
Alexander Kelso Jr.
Stephen Kowalski
Vanessa Lemonides
Emily Lin
Albert Louie
Julian Marshall
Andrea Menotti
Michael Migliacci
Douglas Miller
Julie Mott
Huan "Joe" Nguyen
Karna Nisewaner
James Marc O'Sullivan
Edward Pentz
Thomas Pyle
Cynthia Ray
Michael Richards
Joseph "Jay" Roxe
Arthur Schankler
Morgan Schwartz
Francis Sharry Jr.
Jean-Ju Sheen
Wendy Shreve
Mark Shrime
Jonathan Sichel
Bess Mah Siegal
Leslie Siegel
Katharine Sonnenberg
Annabel Soutar
Marisa Spellman
D. Bruce Stone
David Stricker
Ann Sunhachawee
Luke Tennis
Damon Toth
Thu "Terry" Tran
Christopher Vinnard
Alex Volckhausen
Bruce Von Cannon
Totam "Tammy" Vu
Jeffrey Wall
Carl Walter Jr.
Benjamin Weiss
David Williams
Dorothy Jones Yang
Denis Yu

TAIWAN

Edward Ahnert
Sara Alyea
Grace Ayscue
John Banes
Matthew Bersani
Lawrence Buell
B. Michael Byron
Maria Constantine
Stephanie Crane Guyett
Laura Curtis
Susan Danoff
Stephen Davis
Joseph DeFrisco Jr.
Juliet Douglas
Stephen Douglas
Maram Epstein
David Felsenthal
Gail Tirone Finley
Deborah Forrester
Wendy Gordon-Rockefeller
Florence Gramignano
Elizabeth Green
Douglas Greenig
Mary Greenwald
Michael Herbst
Richard Johnston Jr.
Albert Keidel III
John Langlois Jr.
Jane S. C. Lee
William Leverett
Robert Levy
Laura Lewis
Peter R. Lighte
Lewis Lukens
Michele Mack
Allison Mankin
Gary Martin
David May
Jonathan Miller
Roger Clark Mills
Robert Minor
Katharyne Mitchell
Ann Mongoven
Carla Morreale
Margaret Moss
Jonathan Nicholas
Patricia O'Beirne
Michael Olds
Lynn Paine
Howard Phifer Jr.
Peter Prugh
Claudia Pucci
Albert Redway III
Sheila McNamara Riley
Frank Schwab
Scott Seligman
William 'Lawrence' Severt
Jan Shelburne
Jane Simoni
Iness Snider
Timothy Steinert
Garland Sweitzer
Christopher Thomforde
Frank Upham III
William Volckhausen
Richard Wainstein
Robert Ward
Fannie Cromwell Watkinson
Robert Wolf
Robert Woll
Jon Wonnell
Annette Young

THAILAND

Charles Allen
Francesco Barbera
Kurt Bedell
Leslie Bienen
Dana Bigelow
Ellen Boccuzzi
Susan Bramley
John Brandon
John Buchanan
Sean Callahan
Heather Cameron
Henry Card
Wayne Cardoni Jr.
Michael Carpenter
Catherine Jo Casey
Richard Casey
Leslie Chang
Alexander Ciepley
Sarah Colby
Jeffrey Cranmer
Paul Linus Cummings
Emily Decker
Daniel Dick
Morgaen Donaldson
Matthew Draper
James Edmunds
Wendy Elman
Katharine Emans
Courtney Engelstein
John Evans
William Eville
Victor Fanucchi
Daniel Fineman
Dylan Ford
Mary Foulk
Nicholas Galli
Jill Forney Gates
Matthew Gordon
Nikki Gordon
Seth Grossman
Kenja Hassan
Margaret Hazlett
Lisa Herb
A. Hartley Hobson
Teresa Holland
Bi-sek Hsiao
Daniel Hunter
Jessica Hunter
Tracy Johnson
Deborah Jones
Todd Jones
Megan Katz
Priya Khosla
Alexandra Knoop
Nicholas Kohler
Catarina Krizancic
Julie Lamb
Kathryn Law
Gina Lucarelli
Thomas MacFarlane
Kenneth Maclean
Kristin MacLeod
William Maeck
Emily Daniell Magruder
Lydia Marti
Justine Koeppen McIntosh
David Merchant
Sarah Meek
William Andrew Mims
Jennifer Mulholland
Sandra Musumeci
Peter Nosek
Alexandra Nyberg
Timothy O'Connell
Jessica Pancoast
Mary Park
Jason Pearson
Christopher Peltier
Mark Perlmutter
Van Meter Pettit
Nicholas Phillips
Matthew Pickens
Susan Pietrzyk
Leslie Platt
Julie Polhemus
Sean Reilly
Melissa Repa
Lisa Revelle
Nicole Robertson
Jay Rosengard
Fiona Ruthven
Jon Sarnoff
Karalene Schaupp
Daniel Segal
Joel Selcher
Rebecca Shults
Frank Silverstein
Matthew Simons
Cheryl Smith
Sengsouvanh Soukamneuth
Craig Stuart
Anna Sumner
Mark Thompson
Nicholas Van Dusen
John Read Vanderbilt
Elizabeth Vederman
Chris Ward
Marc Wathen
Lesley Williams
Elise Wilson
Philip Witte

TURKEY

Daniel Golden
W. Scott Trees

UNITED ARAB EMIRATES

David Johnson

VIETNAM

Lily Chiu
Trinh Huynh
Katherine Kaneko
Genevieve Lakier
Margaret McKee
Laura O'Neill
Catholyn Pickup
Steven Prior
Denise Ryan
Margaret Williams

YEMEN

D. Thomas Gochenour III
Virginia Vogt

Art and Photography credits:
The Qing Dynasty painting on the front cover and page 12 is from the collection of The Metropolitan Museum of Art, anonymous gift, 1952. (52.209.3C). Photograph © 1980 The Metropolitan Museum of Art.
The photograph of the bronze tiger at Princeton on page 6 is by Robert P. Matthews. Photographs of Sidney Gamble on pages 16, 19, 20, 21 are courtesy of The Sidney D. Gamble Foundation for China Studies. Bill Bradley photo on page 24 is courtesy of Princeton University.
The Japanese Ganku tiger on page 8 is from The Metropolitan Museum of Art, Rogers Fund, 1936. (36.100.11). Photograph © 1981 The Metropolitan Museum of Art.
The photograph of the Korean tiger carving on page 22 is by Michael Freeman/Corbis Images.
The Japanese Juroku-Rakan on page 34 is from the collection of Art Resource, New York..
The photograph of the painting of Shiva's family on page 44 is by Angelo Hornak/Corbis Images.
The ricefield photograph on page 59 is by Joseph Sohm; ChromoSohm, Inc./Corbis Images.
The Confucian analect and Chinese characters were translated by the East Asian Studies Department of Princeton University. Other art and photographs are from the archives or provided by alumni of Princeton-in-Asia.

Colophon:
Printing is by Dai Nippon America, manufactured in Hong Kong.
Text paperstock is 150gsm Biberist Demi Matte acid-free paper. Bookcloth is Japanese Saifu. Text typography is Fenice Condensed; headlines and sub-heads for text and sidebars are set in Bauer Bondoni; sidebars are set in Univers 47; captions are set in Garamond Condensed Italic.